Critical Acclaim for other books in the How It Works Series

How Networks Work

"Succinctly described and beautifully illustrated..."

—**Eric Cohen,** *Rochester Business Journal*

How to Use Your Computer

"Every so often a wonderful book appears...This is one."
  "...a truly beautiful book comes along that you want to show to anyone you can. Lisa Biow neither insults your intelligence nor assumes that information about computers is hard to grasp. Her explanations are clear and the book is fun to read. And the pictures...are beautiful."

—**Barbara Berger, Pasco Area Computer Users Group Newsletter**

"Lisa Biow...has obviously taken great pains to understand what new users go through. It gives the essential explanations and a little more, leaving further research to the reader. However, it is more than enough to get users started."

—**Madhulika Dayal,** *PC WEEK Asia*

PC/Computing How Computers Work

"As an enjoyable way to learn what makes your system tick, nothing comes close to *How Computers Work*. Browse through it for an entertaining and informative diversion, or work your way through from cover to cover for a thorough orientation. And when you're finished, don't hide it away on some remote shelf—leave it out on your coffee table where everyone can enjoy this beautiful book."

—**Alfred Poor,** *PC Magazine*

"A 'real' book, and quite a handsome one...The artwork, by Mr. Timothy Edward Downs, is striking and informative, and the text by Mr. White, executive editor of [*PC/Computing*], is very lucid."

—**L.R. Shannon,** *New York Times*

"Read [*PC/Computing*] *How Computers Work* to learn about the innerworkings of the IBM and PC-compatible."

—**Ronald Rosenberg,** *Boston Globe*

"...a magnificently seamless integration of text and graphics that makes the complicated physics of the personal computer seem as obvious as gravity. When a book really pleases you—and this one does—there's a tendency to gush, so let's put it this way: I haven't seen any better explanations written (including my own) of how a PC works and why."

—**Larry Blasko, The Associated Press**

"If you're curious but fear computerese might get in the way, this book's the answer...it's an accessible, informative introduction that spreads everything out for logical inspection.

To make everything even clearer, White introduces the explanatory diagrams with a few concise, lucid paragraphs of text. Readers will come away knowing not only what everything looks like but also what it does."

—Stephanie Zvirin, *Booklist*

"...the text in *How Computers Work* is remarkably free of jargon and distractions. Readers are left with a basic impression of how a particular component woks; they're not overloaded with information they may never use or remember...For most PC users, the brief introduction to the subject of disk caching in *How Computers Work* is all they need to understand the basics behind the technology. This is a boon to readers who may have been totally stumped by a more technical description of the process, and who may have avoided the more indepth article. Whether you're new to computers or want a refresher course in the latest technology, *How Computers Work* offers a solid and colorful introduction."

—Gordon McComb, Copley News Service

"Computer users at all levels will enjoy and profit from this book."

—Don Mills, *Computing Now!*

"From mouse to CD-ROM, the treatment manages to convey 'how it works' without being simplistic or overly complex. A very good overview for those curious about how computers make their magic."

—Reference & Research Book News

How to Use
EXCEL

How to Use
EXCEL

Make Microsoft Excel 5.0 Work for You

ERIC STONE

With illustrations by
DAVE FEASEY AND CHERIE PLUMLEE

Ziff-Davis Press
Emeryville, California

Development Editor	Valerie Haynes Perry
Copy Editors	Noelle Graney and Kelly Green
Technical Reviewer	Heidi Steele
Project Coordinator	Kim Haglund
Proofreader	Cort Day
Cover Illustration	Dave Feasey and Cherie Plumlee
Cover Design	Carrie English
Book Design	Dennis Gallagher/Visual Strategies, San Francisco
Screen Graphics Editor	Dan Brodnitz
Technical Illustration	Dave Feasey and Cherie Plumlee Computer Graphics and Illustration
Word Processing	Howard Blechman and Cat Haglund
Page Layout	M.D. Barrera and Bruce Lundquist
Indexer	Valerie Haynes Perry

Ziff-Davis Press books are produced on a Macintosh computer system with the following applications: FrameMaker®, Microsoft® Word, QuarkXPress®, Adobe Illustrator®, Adobe Photoshop®, Adobe Streamline™, MacLink® *Plus*, Aldus® Free-Hand™, Collage Plus™.

Ziff-Davis Press
5903 Christie Avenue
Emeryville, CA 94608
1-800-688-0448

ISBN 1-56276-185-4

Manufactured in the United States of America
10 9 8 7 6 5 4 3 2 1

TABLE OF CONTENTS

100%

ACKNOWLEDGMENTS

 This book "works" because it communicates through graphics as well as words. For the book's graphical effectiveness I heartily thank illustrators Dave Feasey and Cherie Plumlee, designers Carrie English and Dennis Gallagher, layout artists M.D. Barrera and Bruce Lundquist, and screen-shot expert Dan Brodnitz.

Learning guides such as this depend on the smooth flow of ideas and on the consistent, correct use of language. Carefully monitoring and substantially improving the text were development editor Valerie Haynes Perry, technical editor Heidi Steele, copy editors Noelle Graney and Kelly Green, project coordinator Kim Haglund, and proofreader Cort Day.

Many professionals contribute to books in ways that while not obvious to readers, are irreplaceable parts of the publishing process. At Ziff-Davis Press, these people include Elisabeth Beller, Howard Blechman, Charles Cowens, Cat Haglund, Cheryl Holzaepfel, Cori Pansarasa, Joe Schneider, and Simon Tonner. President Harry Blake and publisher Cindy Hudson set this project in motion and provided the inspiration and resources to see it to completion.

Finally, my sincerest thanks go to Tracy Van Hoof of Microsoft Corporation for her timely help, and to Ron White of *PC/Computing* magazine for his defining contributions to the "How It Works" concept.

INTRODUCTION

You're a beginning user of Microsoft Excel 5.0 for Windows. Maybe your math is a little rusty. Maybe you're not even sure what a spreadsheet program is. You're not looking to produce a work of art. You don't need hotshot shortcuts. You just need to get this thing to work.

How to Use Excel is for you. In this concise, colorful book, you will see Excel work right before your eyes, step by step, task by task. When done reading, you will be a comfortable, confident user of the most important features Excel offers. Entering data, performing calculations, creating charts—these indispensable spreadsheet skills and many others will be right at your fingertips.

Each chapter of this book presents up to five related topics. Because each topic spans two facing pages, everything you need to know about a topic is in front of you at one time. Just follow the numbered steps around the pages, reading the text and looking at the pictures. It's really as easy as it looks!

Colorful, realistic examples are included to help you understand how you might use each feature of Excel. You may wish to enter and work with the sample data as you learn, but doing so is not at all mandatory. If you want to stay focused on your own work and use this book as a reference, you will find it well suited for that purpose.

Even experienced computer users occasionally stumble into unfamiliar territory. Read the "Tip Sheet" accompanying each topic to learn more about the occasional pitfall or quirky feature.

You will find special sections called "Try It" at strategic spots in this book. A Try It section is a hands-on exercise that gives you valuable practice with the skills you've acquired to that point. As you read a Try It section, be sure to follow each step at your computer.

To get the most out of this book, read it in sequence. If you have any experience with Microsoft Windows, Microsoft Excel, or electronic spreadsheets in general, you may be familiar with the information in the first three chapters. However, skimming those chapters will provide a useful refresher of important concepts and terms.

I am eager to know your reactions to this book. Please mail any comments and suggestions for future editions to:

Eric Stone
Ziff-Davis Press
5903 Christie Avenue
Emeryville, CA 94608

Welcome aboard.

CHAPTER 1

What Is Electronic Accounting?

 Electronic accounting is the management of financial data on a computer. Before the computer age, accounting was handled on unwieldy paper ledgers. These ponderous documents were understood by few people other than finance experts. Finding information was a challenge. Correcting data and making projections were major undertakings.

With electronic accounting, virtually anyone can understand and manage financial data. It takes just a few commands to find data buried anywhere in the company books. Projections and "what if" analyses take mere moments—and the computer performs all the calculations.

Your personal computer wasn't built with the ability to perform electronic accounting—or to do much of anything else. Just as a CD player needs CDs to make music, a computer needs *programs* to tell it what to do. A program that enables you to perform electronic accounting on your computer is called a *spreadsheet program,* and the data it manages is called a *spreadsheet.* Your computer probably also runs other programs such as word processors, databases, and games.

This book teaches you how to use one spreadsheet program: Excel for Windows, version 5.0, from Microsoft Corporation of Redmond, Washington. Excel for Windows, usually called simply "Excel," is widely regarded as one of the best spreadsheet programs around. Read on to find out why.

What Can a Spreadsheet Program Do?

E lectronic spreadsheets vary in their capabilities, but almost all of them can help you manage and present data like that shown here. This relatively simple spreadsheet highlights many of the once-difficult things that spreadsheet programs do routinely. Let's take a closer look.

1 Most fundamentally, a spreadsheet program gives you an on-screen grid to work with. Each box in the grid (the intersection of a row and a column) is called a *cell*. Most of the time you will put numbers in cells, but sometimes you will enter text, such as column and row headings.

6 Finding data is a cinch. Tell your spreadsheet program you want the name of every department that spent more than $5000 last quarter, and it will pluck this information without batting an eye.

2nd Qtr Totals > $5,000	
Dept.	**Total**
R & D	$8,094
Sales	$12,853

5 A modern spreadsheet program can instantly express your data as a graph. You need know very little about graphing to take advantage of this capability.

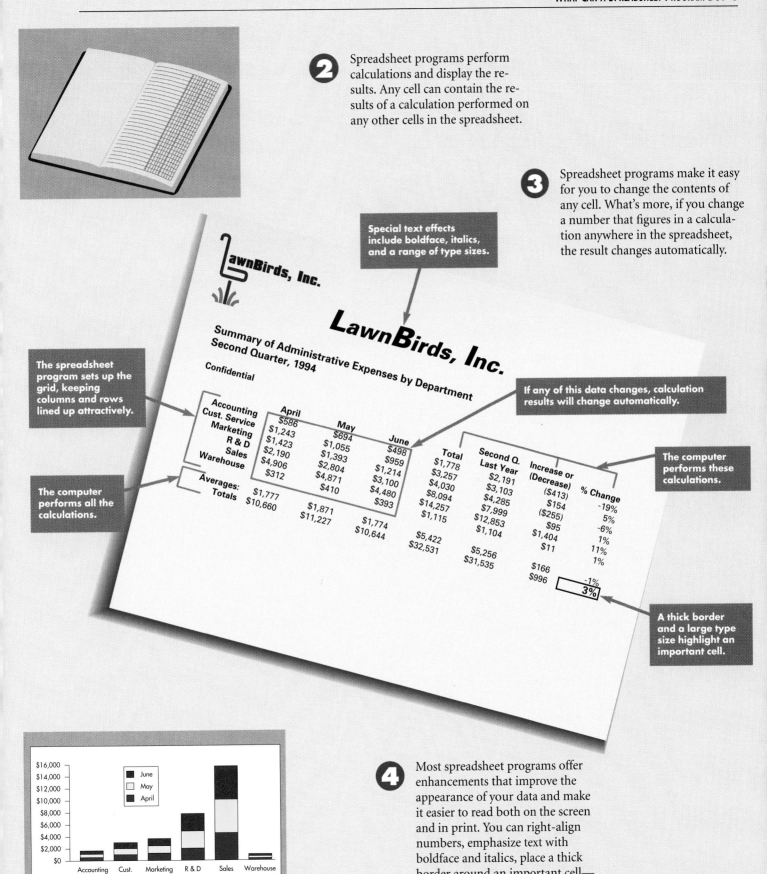

2 Spreadsheet programs perform calculations and display the results. Any cell can contain the results of a calculation performed on any other cells in the spreadsheet.

3 Spreadsheet programs make it easy for you to change the contents of any cell. What's more, if you change a number that figures in a calculation anywhere in the spreadsheet, the result changes automatically.

Special text effects include boldface, italics, and a range of type sizes.

The spreadsheet program sets up the grid, keeping columns and rows lined up attractively.

If any of this data changes, calculation results will change automatically.

The computer performs all the calculations.

The computer performs these calculations.

A thick border and a large type size highlight an important cell.

LawnBirds, Inc.

LawnBirds, Inc.

Summary of Administrative Expenses by Department
Second Quarter, 1994
Confidential

	April	May	June	Total	Second Q. Last Year	Increase or (Decrease)	% Change
Accounting	$586	$694	$498	$1,778	$2,191	($413)	-19%
Cust. Service	$1,243	$1,055	$959	$3,257	$3,103	$154	5%
Marketing	$1,423	$1,393	$1,214	$4,030	$4,285	($255)	-6%
R & D	$2,190	$2,804	$3,100	$8,094	$7,999	$95	1%
Sales	$4,906	$4,871	$4,480	$14,257	$12,853	$1,404	11%
Warehouse	$312	$410	$393	$1,115	$1,104	$11	1%
Averages:	$1,777	$1,871	$1,774	$5,422	$5,256	$166	-1%
Totals	$10,660	$11,227	$10,644	$32,531	$31,535	$996	**3%**

4 Most spreadsheet programs offer enhancements that improve the appearance of your data and make it easier to read both on the screen and in print. You can right-align numbers, emphasize text with boldface and italics, place a thick border around an important cell— and much more.

Excel Is Your Spreadsheet Program

Excel is a product—a brand, if you will. Just as there are different soft drinks on the market, many quite similar, so there are various spreadsheet programs, many excellent but none plainly superior. However, Excel has gained popularity among both beginning and experienced users because of its comfortable "look and feel" and its convenient, versatile features, many of which you'll master as you read this book. You may have heard of other spreadsheet programs such as Lotus 1-2-3 and Quattro Pro. These products compete with Excel for the hearts and dollars of people who perform electronic accounting.

1 Excel is not built into your computer. You buy Excel and install it on your computer much as you buy a CD and insert it in your CD player to play it. It might *seem* like Excel was built into your computer if someone else installed it on the computer's hard disk for you, or if you use a copy that's installed on your office network.

TIP SHEET

▶ This book is about version 5.0 of Microsoft Excel for Windows. Unless you have version 5.0, you cannot be sure that everything you read in this book applies to you. Check your Excel packaging to verify the version number if you're not sure of it.

▶ Chapter 2 of this book is for first-time computer users or first-time Windows users. If you can start Microsoft Windows, use the mouse, select commands from a menu, and make selections in a dialog box, skip ahead to Chapter 3. If you can't do all these things (or if you don't even know what they mean!), you'd best not skip ahead.

6 You give instructions to Excel in one of two ways: by typing, or by using the *mouse*, a hand-held pointing device. Excel does not absolutely require the use of the mouse, but it sure encourages it. See "How to Use the Mouse in Windows" in Chapter 2 if you are a first-time mouse user.

2 Excel is based on Microsoft Windows, a program that helps you manage the computing environment and run other programs. This means that Excel's *interface* (the way you give commands to it and receive information from it) is similar to that of many other programs, including some you may already know how to use.

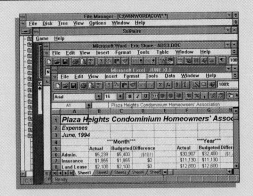

3 Excel is quite well regarded. Many spreadsheet experts—and ordinary users, too—consider it the finest Windows-based spreadsheet program. You'll be using a program that has withstood the test of time and earned the respect of the computing community.

4 What makes Excel such a standout? Well, it has lots of useful features and plenty of convenient shortcuts for expert users. But most users, especially beginners, would answer in less tangible terms: "It's easy," or, "It feels right."

5 Excel is a spreadsheet program, and it sports the same basic features as other modern spreadsheet programs. Like the other programs, it helps you manage, analyze, and present financial data.

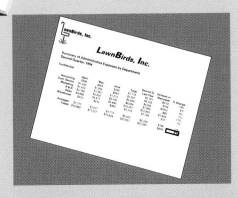

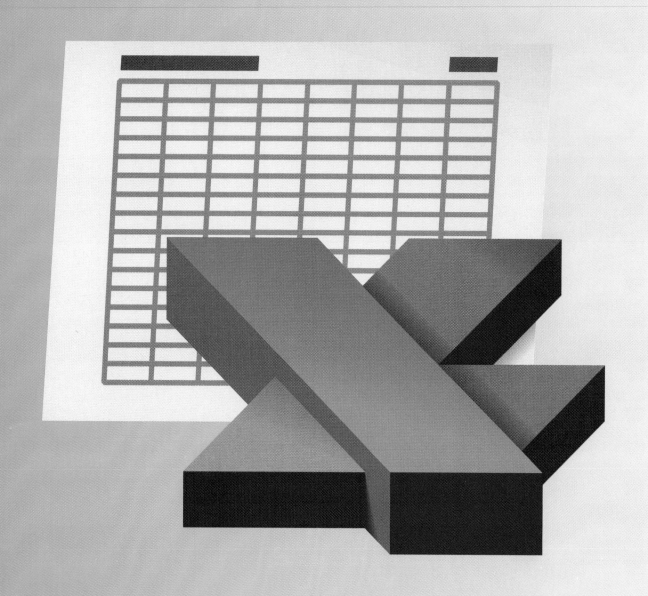

CHAPTER 2

What Are DOS and Windows?

 DOS and Windows are programs that enable you to run all the programs you really *want* to run: your spreadsheet (Excel), your word processor, your games, and so on.

DOS, short for *disk operating system,* moves information to and from the disks in your computer. Without an operating system, your computer cannot do anything useful for you. You cannot run a program like Excel unless you tell DOS to move it temporarily from the disk into *random-access memory* (RAM), a storage area that your computer can interact with quickly and directly. Likewise, you cannot electronically store and later reuse your data unless you have DOS copy it from RAM onto a disk.

Windows can simplify your role in directing these and many other affairs on your computer. It also provides a consistent and fairly appealing backdrop for Windows-based programs such as Excel. Windows-based programs look comfortingly similar on the screen, and there are many similarities in the ways you work with them. If you've used any Windows-based program, certain Excel operations will be familiar to you.

You don't need to start DOS. It is running whenever you are using your computer. Windows, on the other hand, is an add-on program that you have the option of running as you use your computer. But Windows *must* be running before you can start Excel or any other Windows-based program. This chapter helps you start and run Windows. If you already know how to start Windows and use any Windows-based program, you can safely skip this chapter.

How to Start Windows from DOS

The heart and soul of DOS, at least from the user's viewpoint, is the *DOS prompt.* This is where DOS asks you for information and you provide it. By typing *commands* at the DOS prompt, you can run programs, check the contents of your disks, reset the time on your computer's internal clock, and much more. For now, the only DOS command you absolutely must know is the one to start Windows.

1 Switch on your computer and give it a minute or so to go through its wake-up ritual. When the computer is ready to accept information from you, it will ask you for the information or display the DOS prompt.

TIP SHEET

▶ **Your computer may be set up to bypass the DOS prompt and start Windows automatically. If Windows has started, you'll see the words *Program Manager* somewhere on the screen. In this case, you can skip steps 4 and 5—whose purpose is, after all, to help you start Windows.**

▶ **Upon startup, some computers automatically run the *DOS Shell,* an interface designed to make DOS operations easier. If your computer is running the DOS Shell, you'll see the words *MS-DOS Shell* across the top of the screen. Hold down the Alt key as you type fx to exit the DOS Shell and face the DOS prompt. Then proceed with step 4.**

▶ **A consultant or office computer specialist may have set up a *custom menu* that appears in place of the DOS prompt. This menu should contain an entry for *Windows* (or possibly *Microsoft Windows* or *Windows 3.1* or a similar variation). To start Windows, you probably have to press the ↓ key until the Windows entry is highlighted, and then press Enter. However, you may have to consult with your consultant or office computer specialist to learn how the custom menu works.**

5 If the preceding step produced a message such as *Bad command or file name,* try typing **c:\windows\win** and pressing Enter. If that fails, try **d:\windows\win**. Still can't start Windows? Well, the possible reasons and solutions are too many to enumerate here, but a computer-savvy colleague should be able to help you in short order. Or call Microsoft technical support, which fields questions like yours routinely.

2 Provide any information the computer asks for, and press the Enter key when done. Some computers ask for the date and time. If your computer is on a *network*—a setup where personal computers in an office are hooked together to share information—it may ask you for your name and password. (Your office's network administrator can help you with this step.)

3 After providing any initial information your computer needs, you see the DOS prompt. This is the way DOS asks you to give it a command. The most common DOS prompt looks like *C:\>* but it can vary considerably. You can easily start Windows no matter how the DOS prompt looks.

4 Type **win** and press the Enter key. On most computers, this command will start Windows. After a few seconds, you'll see *Program Manager* somewhere on the screen, indicating that Windows is now running. Skip the next step if this step worked fine.

How to Start a Program from Program Manager

*P*rogram Manager is a Windows-based program that comes with Windows. Its role is to make it easy to start *other* programs, including Excel. Program Manager is like your home base; it opens when you start Windows and remains open as long as Windows is running. This picture shows how Program Manager might look when you start Windows. Then again, Windows is highly customizable, so your starting screen can look quite different.

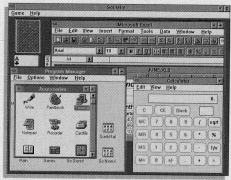

1 A window is simply an on-screen box containing information. Like most Windows-based programs, Program Manager has an application window and lets you open multiple document windows inside it. In this screen there are six windows wholly or partially visible, as represented by six title bars.

Menu bar

Application window

Document window

TIP SHEET

▶ **To open a program group window using the keyboard, press the Alt key, type w to pull down the Window menu, and type the number next to the program group you want to open. To start a program using the keyboard, open its program group window, use the arrow keys to highlight the name of the program, and press Enter.**

▶ **Under Windows, you can have more than one program running at a time. After starting one program, press Alt+Esc (hold down Alt, press and release Esc, and release Alt) to return to Program Manager. Then find and start the next program. Use the Alt+Esc key combination to switch among all your open programs.**

▶ **To close a window, double-click on the** *Control Menu box* **in the window's upper-left corner. Closing an application window this way shuts down the program. Closing the Program Manager application window closes Windows and returns you to the DOS prompt.**

Double-click to start the Paintbrush program.

6 Then, to start a program, locate its program item in a program group window, roll the mouse to point to the program name or icon, and double-click.

5 When you want to start a program, first open the program group window containing its program item. To open a program group window, roll the mouse until the arrow points to the group name or icon, and then click the left mouse button twice in rapid succession ("double-click").

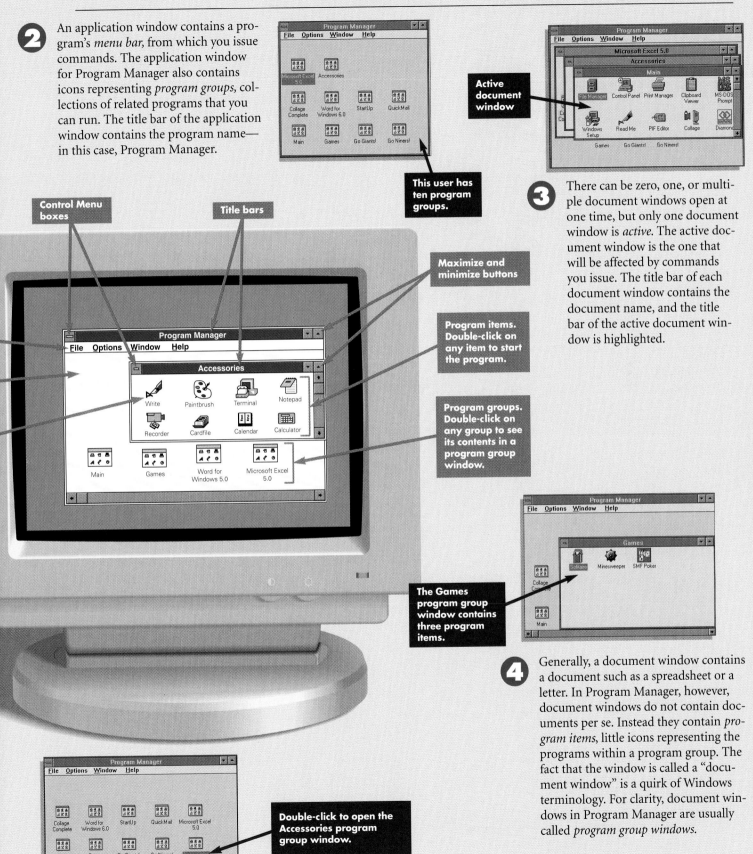

2 An application window contains a program's *menu bar*, from which you issue commands. The application window for Program Manager also contains icons representing *program groups*, collections of related programs that you can run. The title bar of the application window contains the program name—in this case, Program Manager.

This user has ten program groups.

Active document window

3 There can be zero, one, or multiple document windows open at one time, but only one document window is *active*. The active document window is the one that will be affected by commands you issue. The title bar of each document window contains the document name, and the title bar of the active document window is highlighted.

Control Menu boxes

Title bars

Maximize and minimize buttons

Program items. Double-click on any item to start the program.

Program groups. Double-click on any group to see its contents in a program group window.

The Games program group window contains three program items.

4 Generally, a document window contains a document such as a spreadsheet or a letter. In Program Manager, however, document windows do not contain documents per se. Instead they contain *program items*, little icons representing the programs within a program group. The fact that the window is called a "document window" is a quirk of Windows terminology. For clarity, document windows in Program Manager are usually called *program group windows*.

Double-click to open the Accessories program group window.

How to Use the Mouse in Windows

An *input device* is a means of giving instructions to the computer. You're probably familiar with the keyboard as the most common input device. A *mouse,* so named for its hunched-over appearance and tail-like cable, is a hand-held input device that along with the keyboard is one of the two input devices most people use routinely in Windows. Although it's possible to get by without a mouse and do all your work from the keyboard, it's not too wise. The Windows interface was designed with the mouse in mind. Keyboard alternatives can be awkward—and it's not always easy to find out what they are. Take a few minutes to learn the major mouse moves and you'll reward yourself with smoother computing.

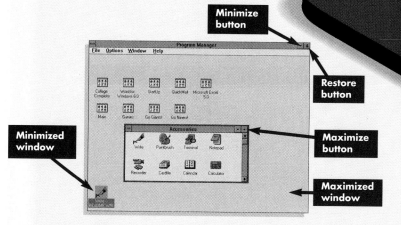

The mouse pointer is on the Write program icon.

1 To *roll* the mouse means to move the mouse along the table-top without pressing one of the mouse buttons. As you roll the mouse, the *mouse pointer* on the screen moves in the same direction. You only roll the mouse to "point to" something on the screen as a prelude to another action.

Minimize button

Restore button

Maximize button

Minimized window

Maximized window

6 To *maximize* a window (enlarge it so it fills the screen), click on its maximize button. To *restore* a maximized window to its original size, click on its restore button. To *minimize* a window so it's merely an icon with a title, click on its minimize button. To restore a minimized window to its original size, double-click on its title or icon.

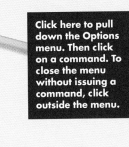

Click here to pull down the Options menu. Then click on a command. To close the menu without issuing a command, click outside the menu.

2 To *click* on something means to point to it (roll the mouse so the mouse pointer is on top of it) and then press and instantly release the left mouse button. To *double-click* on something means to point to it and then click the left mouse button twice in rapid succession.

Drag across a word to select it. Then press the Delete key to delete it.

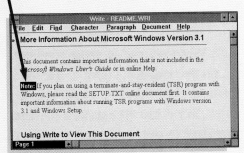

3 To *drag* the mouse means to point to something, press and *hold down* the left mouse button, roll the mouse, and then release the mouse button. For example, you can "select" a block of text for deletion by dragging from one end of the block to the other.

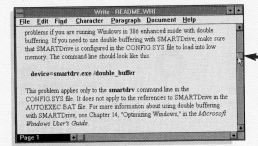

4 *Scrolling* is one of the most common mouse actions. When a document window cannot accommodate all its contents at once, point to a scroll arrow and hold down the left mouse button to "scroll" the display in the direction of the arrow.

We are about one-quarter of the way through the document. Drag the scroll button along the scroll bar to see the rest of the document.

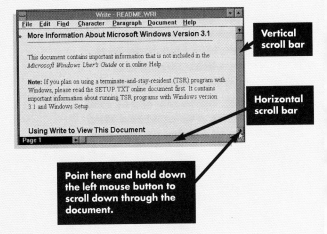

Vertical scroll bar

Horizontal scroll bar

Point here and hold down the left mouse button to scroll down through the document.

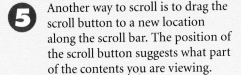

5 Another way to scroll is to drag the scroll button to a new location along the scroll bar. The position of the scroll button suggests what part of the contents you are viewing.

How to Use the Keyboard in Windows

In Windows and in most Windows-based programs, you don't have to use the keyboard for much of anything—except, of course, to type text. But if you type quite a bit, you may be interested in optional ways to issue commands, move through documents such as spreadsheets, and perform other common actions without having to reach for the mouse. The more experience you get in a Windows-based program, the more likely you'll hanker for keyboard alternatives to the mouse actions you perform most often. Even if you're a true mouse-o-phile, you should be aware of the major keyboard techniques in case your mouse ever malfunctions.

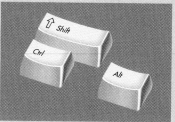

1 The Shift, Alt, and Ctrl keys always work in combination with other keys. No doubt you know that pressing the Shift key along with a letter key types a capital letter. Shift, Alt, and Ctrl can combine with practically any key on your keyboard.

7 Not surprisingly, the Escape key (Esc on most keyboards) lets you slam the door on possible hazards. If you pull down a menu but decide not to issue a command, press Escape twice to deactivate the menu bar. If you issue a command and a dialog box appears (see next page) but you don't want to proceed, press Escape to close the dialog box.

6 To pull down a menu from the menu bar, press Alt and then type the underlined character in the menu name. For example, in Program Manager press Alt and type o to pull down the Options menu. Then, to issue a command from the menu, type the underlined character in the command name.

TIP SHEET

▶ In many programs, the PgUp and PgDn keys scroll the window contents in large increments, Ctrl+Home moves to the top of the window contents, and Ctrl+End moves to the bottom.

▶ Your function keys may be across the top of the keyboard or along the left side. Function keys along the side are easier for touch typists to reach and may make it worthwhile to memorize some keyboard shortcuts in your favorite programs.

2 Most often, Shift, Alt, and Ctrl combine with the *function keys,* labeled F1 through F10 or F12, as an alternative way to issue a command. For example, in most Windows programs, press Alt+F4 (hold down Alt, press and release F4, and release Alt) to close the program.

3 When you don't want to reach for the mouse to scroll through the contents of a window, use the ↑, ↓, →, and ← keys instead. Some keyboards have a separate set of arrow keys, while others have only the arrow keys on the numeric keypad. If the arrows on the numeric keypad don't work, press the Num Lock key and they should work fine.

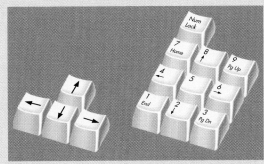

4 Press the Caps Lock key to type a series of uppercase letters without holding down Shift, and press Caps Lock again to switch it off when you're done typing in uppercase. Press the Num Lock key to use the numeric keypad for typing numbers rather than for scrolling, and press Num Lock again to switch off this feature.

Type the underlined character to issue the command.

Control menu of the Accessories document window

5 To maximize, minimize, restore, or close a window, first open its Control menu. Press Alt+spacebar to open the Control menu of an application window; press Alt+hyphen to open the Control menu of a document window. Use the ↓ key to highlight the command you want: Maximize, Minimize, Restore, or Close. Then press Enter.

How to Talk to a Dialog Box

A *dialog box* is where you give Windows (or a Windows-based program) the information it needs to carry out a command you have issued. Say you issue a command called Print, a command found in many programs. Before doing any printing, the program may present a dialog box to ask you how much of the window contents to print, how many copies to print, what printer to print it on, and so forth. Once you answer, the Print command takes effect. The name *dialog box* is slightly misleading. In a human dialog, the participants take turns speaking. In a computerized dialog, the program asks all its questions at once, and then you give all your answers. It's more like a questionnaire than a dialog.

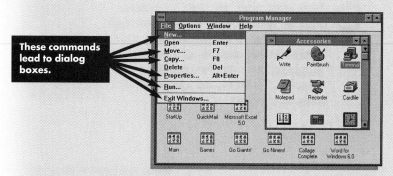

These commands lead to dialog boxes.

1 In Windows menus, the presence of three dots after a command name means that a dialog box will appear when you issue the command. Some dialog boxes are small while others take up most of the screen. It depends on how many questions the program needs to ask.

TIP SHEET

▶ To choose a dialog box option from the keyboard, hold down Alt and type the underlined character in the option name. If the dialog box lacks underlined characters, press Tab to move from option to option. Then, to mark or clear a check box, press the spacebar. To mark the desired radio button within a group, use the arrow keys. To drop down a list, press the down arrow key; then press the down arrow to highlight your choice, and press Tab.

▶ If you need to see what's behind a dialog box, move the box by dragging its title bar.

▶ To close a dialog box without issuing the command, click on the Cancel button (available in most dialog boxes), double-click on the box's Control Menu box, or press Escape.

OK

6 When you've provided all the information requested, issue the command by clicking on the button labeled OK or on another appropriately named button. (The button name might be Print or Find or something else related to the command.)

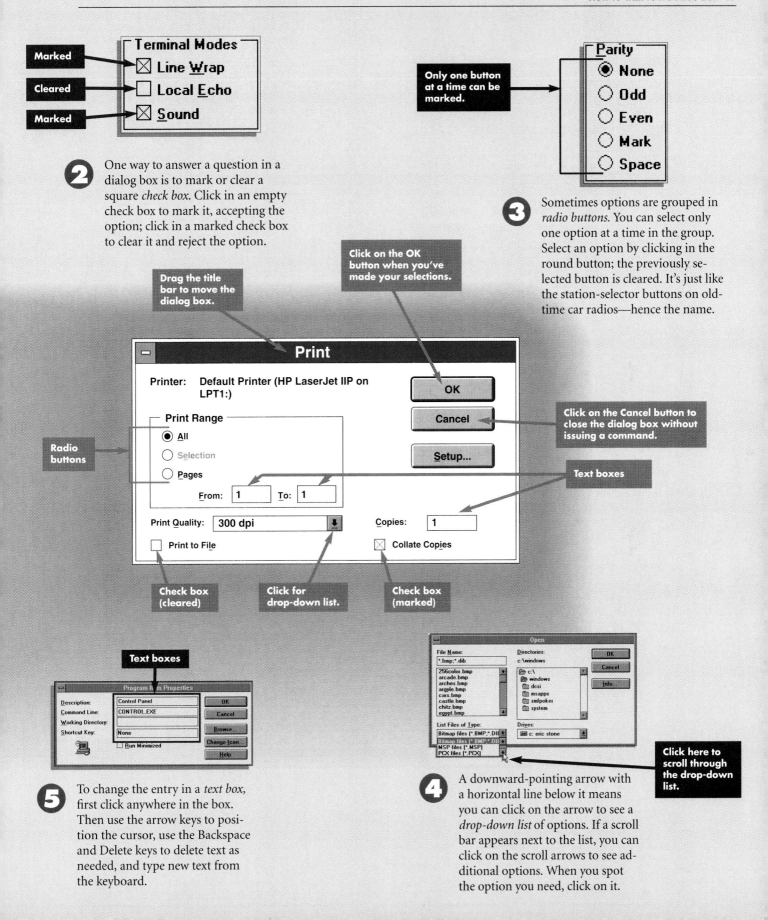

Marked → ⊠ Line **W**rap

Cleared → ☐ Local **E**cho

Marked → ⊠ **S**ound

Terminal Modes

Only one button at a time can be marked. →

Parity

⦿ **None**

○ **O**dd

○ **E**ven

○ **M**ark

○ **S**pace

2 One way to answer a question in a dialog box is to mark or clear a square *check box*. Click in an empty check box to mark it, accepting the option; click in a marked check box to clear it and reject the option.

3 Sometimes options are grouped in *radio buttons*. You can select only one option at a time in the group. Select an option by clicking in the round button; the previously selected button is cleared. It's just like the station-selector buttons on old-time car radios—hence the name.

Drag the title bar to move the dialog box.

Click on the OK button when you've made your selections.

Print

Printer: Default Printer (HP LaserJet IIP on LPT1:)

OK

Cancel

Click on the Cancel button to close the dialog box without issuing a command.

Print Range

⦿ **A**ll

○ Selection

○ **P**ages

From: 1   To: 1

Setup...

Radio buttons →

Text boxes

Print Quality: 300 dpi ▼   Cop**i**es: 1

☐ Print to **F**ile   ⊠ Collate Cop**i**es

Check box (cleared)   **Click for drop-down list.**   **Check box (marked)**

Text boxes

Program Item Properties

Description: Control Panel

Command Line: CONTROL.EXE

Working Directory:

Shortcut Key: None

☐ Run Minimized

OK

Cancel

Browse...

Change Icon...

Help

Open

File **N**ame:
.bmp;.dib

256color.bmp
arcade.bmp
arches.bmp
argyle.bmp
cars.bmp
castle.bmp
chitz.bmp
egypt.bmp

D**i**rectories:
c:\windows

📁 c:\
  📁 windows
    📁 dcsi
    📁 msapps
    📁 smfpoker
    📁 system

OK
Cancel
Info...

List Files of **T**ype:
Bitmap files (*.BMP;*.DIB
Bitmap files (*.BMP;*.DIB
MSP files (*.MSP)
PCX files (*.PCX)

Dri**v**es:
💾 c: eric stone

Click here to scroll through the drop-down list.

5 To change the entry in a *text box,* first click anywhere in the box. Then use the arrow keys to position the cursor, use the Backspace and Delete keys to delete text as needed, and type new text from the keyboard.

4 A downward-pointing arrow with a horizontal line below it means you can click on the arrow to see a *drop-down list* of options. If a scroll bar appears next to the list, you can click on the scroll arrows to see additional options. When you spot the option you need, click on it.

CHAPTER 3

Welcome to Excel

 Excel operations are based on *worksheets* and *workbooks*. A worksheet is the basic spreadsheet, like a page from an old-fashioned ledger book. It is where you enter and work with related data. A workbook is like the ledger book itself: a set of worksheets. You will find it convenient to keep related worksheets—for example, all of your company's personnel worksheets—in one workbook.

You always get a clean slate when you start Excel for Windows. You can type a new worksheet or redisplay and work with data you entered previously.

Though no data is displayed when you start Excel, your screen is not exactly blank. Rather, it contains an array of tools designed to help you work. Some of these tools, such as the menu bar and the Control Menu boxes, are common to most Windows-based programs. Others are particular to Excel.

As you progress through this book, you will incorporate many of these tools in your work. Other tools are so specialized that you may never use them (and never miss them). One key to learning Excel painlessly is to be undaunted by the large number of tools available. This book will point out the most important tools when you need them. Blissfully ignore the rest.

This chapter briefly introduces you to the environment you'll call home when using Excel. Relax and take a little time to get your bearings!

How to Get Started in Excel

When you start Excel for Windows, you see a maximized application window and a restored (neither maximized nor minimized) document window. The document window is a blank worksheet in a blank workbook containing cells in which you can enter your data.

1 To start Excel, first start Windows. Then open the program group containing Excel and double-click on the Microsoft Excel icon. (See Chapter 2 for help with these operations.)

TIP SHEET

▸ Your opening screen may differ from the one shown here if you or another user has customized your Excel environment. If so, you may wish to reset certain display options so you can better follow the instructions and examples in this book. To do this, click on View in the menu bar and observe the View menu. If there is not a checkmark next to the Formula Bar command, click on this command. Likewise, if the Status Bar command has no checkmark, click on it. If the Full Screen command does have a checkmark, click on this command. Do not worry about other differences between your screen and the ones shown in this book. They will not affect your ability to learn and use Excel.

▸ What you see in the document window when you start Excel is only the top-left corner of the worksheet. An Excel worksheet contains 256 columns and 16,384 rows for a total of 4,194,304 cells! After *Z*, column headings become double letters *AA* through *IV*. Of course, you're not likely to take advantage of the entire available grid, but many worksheets are large enough that you have to scroll the document window to see the part you want to work with.

Ready

8 The *status bar* at the bottom of the screen gives you potentially helpful messages about Excel operations. Now it says *Ready*, meaning simply that Excel is ready for you to enter data in the worksheet. As you issue an Excel command, the status bar briefly describes the command's purpose. The boxes to the right sometimes contain other reminders appropriate to your work situation. For example, if you switch on Caps Lock or Num Lock, this is noted with *CAPS* or *NUM* in the status bar.

7 Notice the shape of the mouse pointer when it is resting over a cell. This shape changes depending on where you are pointing. The meanings of different mouse pointer shapes will be explained throughout this book.

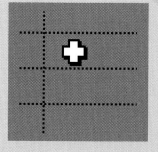

2 Observe the two title bars now on your screen: Microsoft Excel (the application window) and Book1 (the document window). Book1 is a temporary name that Excel uses until you assign a name to the workbook (see Chapter 6).

3 Now observe the menu bar. Excel's menu bar contains nine menu names. To experiment, you can click on any menu name to pull down the menu. Click outside the pulled-down menu to close it without issuing a command.

4 The Standard and Formatting *toolbars* contain optional tools and shortcuts for a variety of Excel commands. Once you have some experience, the toolbars may help you become a more efficient Excel user. For now, ignore the toolbars, and don't worry if your toolbars are different from the ones shown here—or are simply absent. Chapter 15 offers more information.

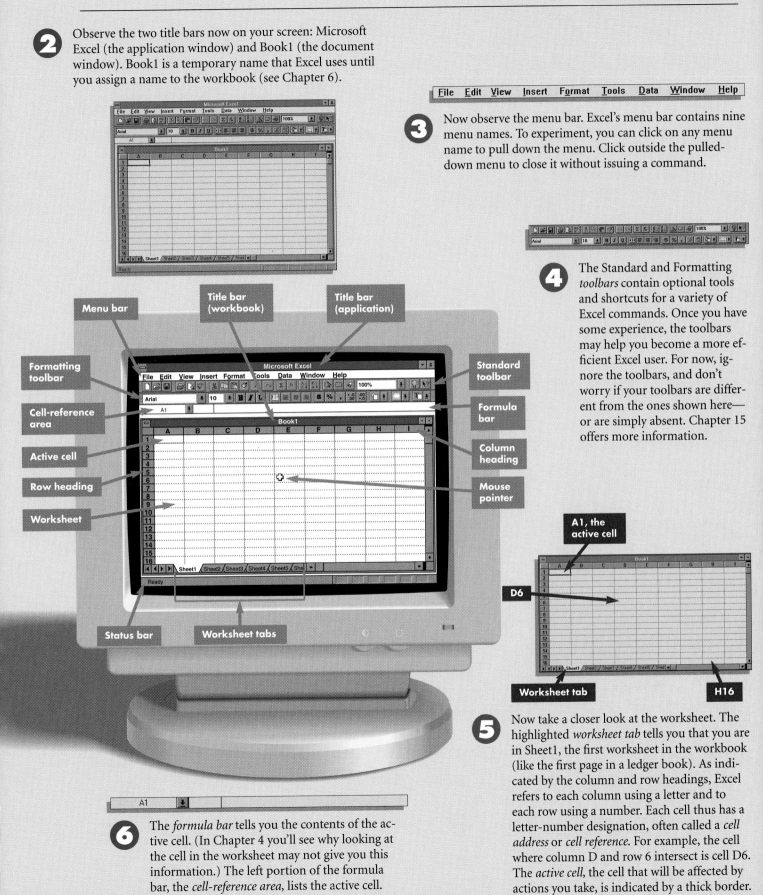

5 Now take a closer look at the worksheet. The highlighted *worksheet tab* tells you that you are in Sheet1, the first worksheet in the workbook (like the first page in a ledger book). As indicated by the column and row headings, Excel refers to each column using a letter and to each row using a number. Each cell thus has a letter-number designation, often called a *cell address* or *cell reference*. For example, the cell where column D and row 6 intersect is cell D6. The *active cell*, the cell that will be affected by actions you take, is indicated by a thick border.

6 The *formula bar* tells you the contents of the active cell. (In Chapter 4 you'll see why looking at the cell in the worksheet may not give you this information.) The left portion of the formula bar, the *cell-reference area*, lists the active cell.

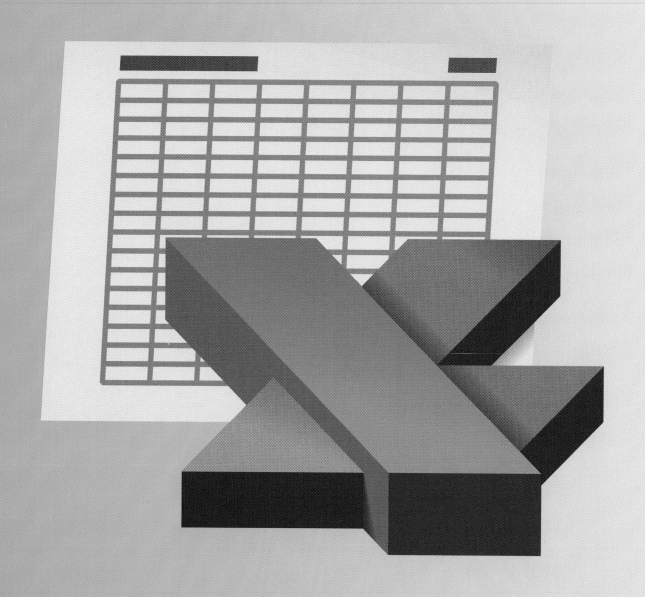

CHAPTER 4

Setting Up a Worksheet

 A workbook containing vital business data is bound to be part of your life for a long time. Therefore, you should plan the structure of each worksheet carefully. A well-planned, well-structured worksheet saves you time and aggravation in two ways. First, it makes data easy to find and work with. And second, it saves you time you might spend restructuring the worksheet later.

What is involved in planning a worksheet? Fundamentally, not much. Decide what data you need to present, what order to present it in, and what operations to perform on it. However, beneath this fundamental simplicity may rest layers of complexity that only you, as the holder of the business data, can fathom. After a few months, today's perfect worksheet may look like a relic from the Dark Ages as accounting codes are revised, departments are added, new reports are requested, and employees come and go.

The upshot: Take some time to think about your data needs *before* firing up Excel. Then, build your worksheet. This chapter is here to help you get started and to make minor changes to your data. What about those inevitable overhauls down the road? Excel makes them quite painless. The techniques you'll need are covered in Chapters 8 and 9.

How to Enter Data

Any time you see the word *Ready* in the status bar, you can enter data in your worksheet. You enter data simply by typing letters, numbers, and punctuation characters from your keyboard. The procedure is the same whether you are entering text (such as a column heading) or a number.

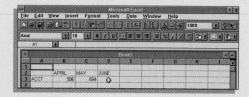

1 Locate the cell where you want to insert data. Use the scroll bars to scroll the cell into view if it is hidden.

TIP SHEET

▶ Since your hands are already on the keyboard (and not on the mouse) as you enter data, you may prefer to press the Enter key rather than click on the enter box to complete an entry. For the same reason, you may prefer to activate a cell by moving onto it with the arrow keys rather than clicking on it.

▶ On most computer systems, when you press the Enter key to complete an entry, the cell selection highlighting jumps down to the cell below. This makes it easier to enter a column of data. Don't worry if Excel does not work this way for you. It simply means that another user customized your system. You can always activate any cell by clicking on it or by moving the cell selection highlighting onto it with the arrow keys.

▶ Excel allows you to enter data that is too wide for the column. However, it may not display the data completely. Regardless of the display, Excel "remembers" your complete entry and restores its display if you widen the column (see Chapter 8). If the entry is a number, Excel will use the complete number in calculations even if the display is incomplete.

▶ See Chapter 5 to learn how to edit cell contents after entering them.

Excel is ready to accept data.

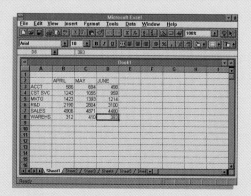

6 Repeat the preceding steps to enter the rest of your data.

Click to activate.

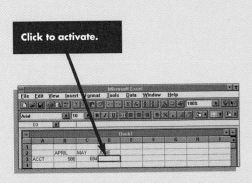

2 Click on the cell to make it the active cell.

Cancel

Enter

Function Wizard

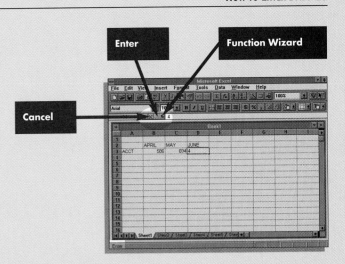

3 Type the cell contents. The text you type appears both in the active cell and in the formula bar. Observe that when you start typing, three buttons appear in the formula bar: the *enter box*, the *cancel box*, and the *Function Wizard box* (see Chapter 10). Observe also that the status bar reads *Enter*.

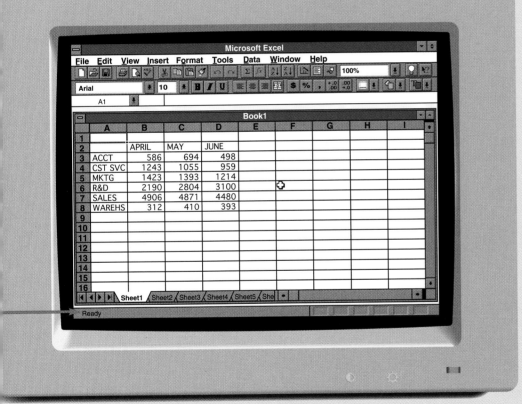

4 Click on the enter box to tell Excel that you are done typing the data. Or, simply press the Enter key. This step is called *entering* the data.

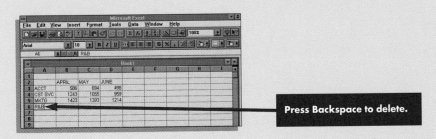

Press Backspace to delete.

5 If you make a mistake while typing data (but before entering it), press the Backspace key to delete the last character. Or, to erase the cell contents and start over, click on the cancel box or press the Escape (Esc) key.

How to Enter a Formula

Much of the magic of electronic spreadsheets is that a cell need not contain fixed data. Instead, a cell can contain a formula that performs a calculation on numeric data anywhere else in the worksheet and displays the result. If you edit the supporting data (see Chapter 5), the result changes automatically.

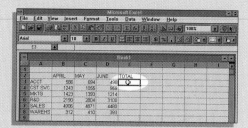

1 Click on the cell where you want to place the formula, making this cell the active cell.

▶ **You cannot tell by looking at a worksheet whether a cell contains a fixed number or the results of a formula. Instead, you must click on the cell to activate it, and then look at the formula bar. The formula bar always shows the underlying contents of a cell.**

▶ **Excel never miscalculates. If the results of a formula are obviously wrong, or if Excel presents an error message, then you typed the formula incorrectly. Common mistakes include forgetting the leading equal sign and mistyping a cell reference. See Chapter 5 to learn how to edit a formula.**

▶ **In cell references, you can type letters in uppercase or lowercase. Excel converts the letters to uppercase when you enter the formula. You can, but need not, type spaces around the mathematical operators.**

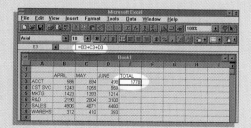

5 Observe that the cell now contains the results of the calculation, but whenever the cell is active, the formula bar shows the underlying formula.

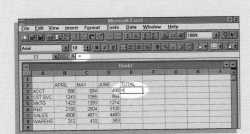

"The contents of cell B3 plus the contents of cell C3 plus the contents of cell D3"

2 Type an equal sign (=).

3 Type the calculation you want to perform, but use cell references instead of the actual numbers stored in the cells where appropriate. That way, if you later revise the numbers in the referenced cells, Excel will redo the calculation based on the new numbers. The mathematical operators available in formulas include + for addition, - for subtraction, * for multiplication, and / for division.

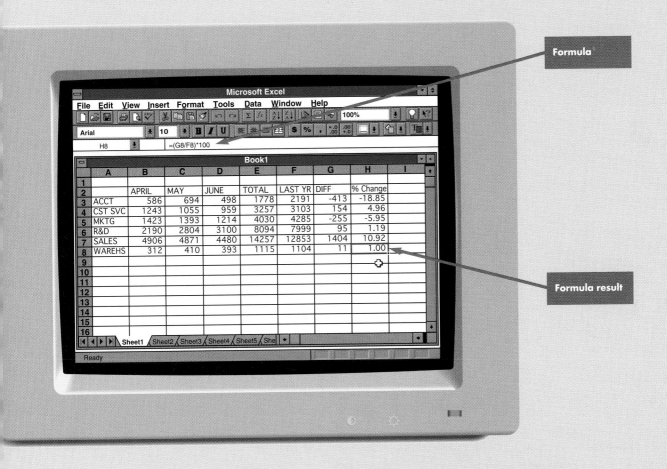

Formula

Formula result

4 Enter the formula by clicking on the enter box or pressing the Enter key.

How to Sum Numbers

On the preceding page you learned one way to calculate the sum of two or more numbers in a worksheet: Construct a formula in which the cells to sum are separated with plus signs. When you must sum quite a few numbers—twelve monthly totals, for example—this can be cumbersome. Happily, Excel offers a SUM function, a built-in formula that produces the same result with less effort and less chance for a typographical error. As you'll see, the SUM function is especially convenient when the numbers to sum are in adjacent cells, either along a row or down a column.

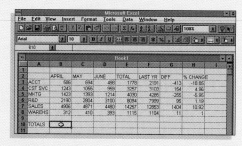

1 Click on the cell where you want the sum to appear.

SUM function

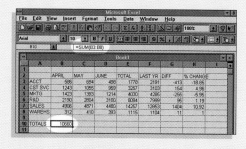

6 Observe that the cell now displays the sum of the numbers in the specified cells, while the formula bar contains the SUM function whenever the cell is active.

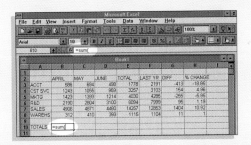

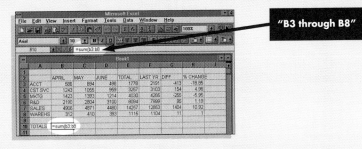

"B3 through B8"

2 Type =**sum**(using lowercase or uppercase.

3 If the cells to sum are adjacent, type the first cell, followed by a colon (:), followed by the last cell. If the cells are not adjacent, simply list the cell references, separating them with commas.

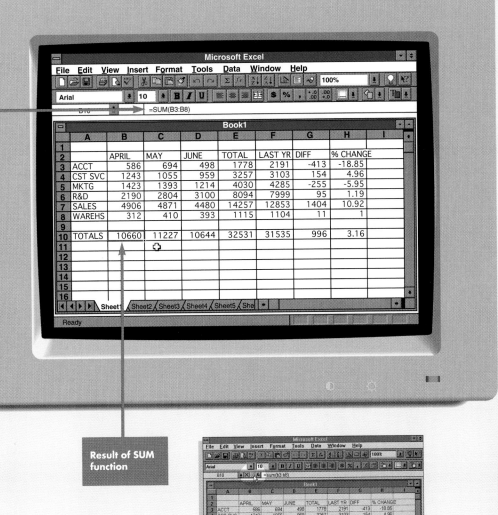

Result of SUM function

4 Type a closing parenthesis:).

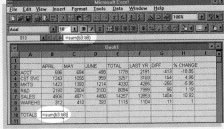

5 Click on the enter box or press the Enter key.

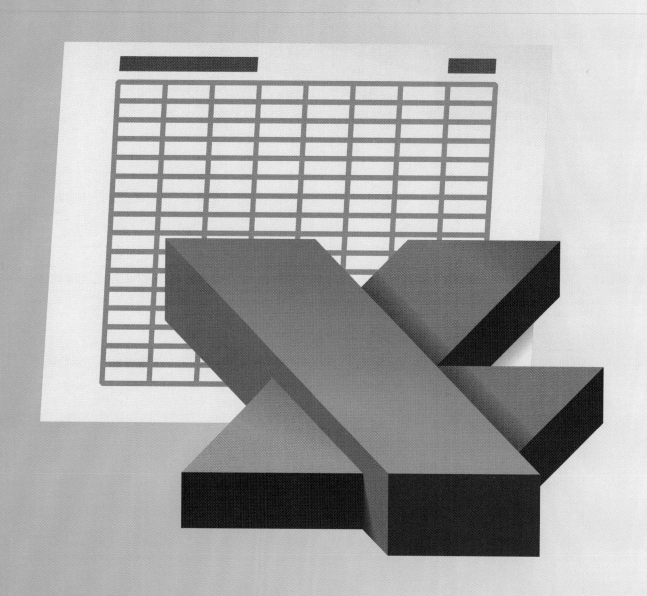

CHAPTER 5

Working with Worksheets

 You don't build a worksheet just to look at it; a worksheet is a tool. It helps you understand your business data, forecast the future, and make decisions.

Using a worksheet requires skills beyond the data and formula entry you have learned so far. What happens when your data change? What if you need to project the impact of possible future data? What about whole new data types—a new department, revised accounting codes, personnel changes?

Anyone who uses an electronic spreadsheet needs certain worksheet maintenance skills. This chapter covers the most fundamental of those skills. In this chapter you will learn how to find your way around a large worksheet, how to edit data, how to project future results ("what-if" analysis), and how to select a group of cells so that you can apply a command to all of them. Future chapters expand and reinforce these important techniques.

How to Move through a Worksheet

Rarely is a worksheet compact enough to fit on the screen all at once. Many Excel worksheets sprawl across dozens of columns and hundreds of rows. For example, a personnel worksheet may contain pay and benefits information for hundreds of employees. A worksheet with a company's financial figures may cover several years, month by month. You already know that you can scroll any part of the worksheet into view and then click on any cell to activate it, or simply move onto a cell using the arrow keys. But there are easier, more efficient ways to move about a large worksheet. Here are the best of them.

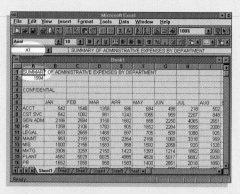

1 To move to cell A1, press Ctrl+Home.

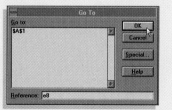

Several rows are out of view.

7 Finally, click on the OK button. The cell you named becomes the active cell.

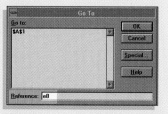

6 Next, in the Reference text box of the Go To dialog box, type the cell to which you want to move.

TIP SHEET

▶ Scrolling does not change the active cell. Therefore, it is possible for the active cell to be out of view. Even in this situation, the formula bar tells you the active cell.

▶ The bottom-right cell in the active area of the worksheet (step 2) is the intersection of the last nonblank row and the last nonblank column in the worksheet. Depending on the worksheet structure, this may be a blank cell.

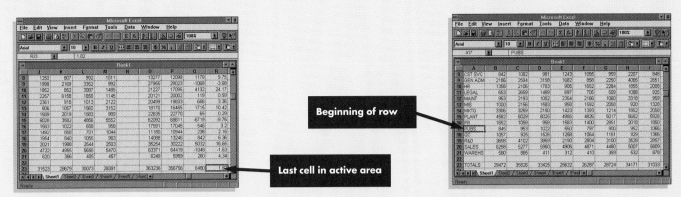

Beginning of row

Last cell in active area

2 To move to the bottom-right cell in the active area of the worksheet, press Ctrl+End.

3 To move to the beginning of the current row, press Home.

Several columns are out of view.

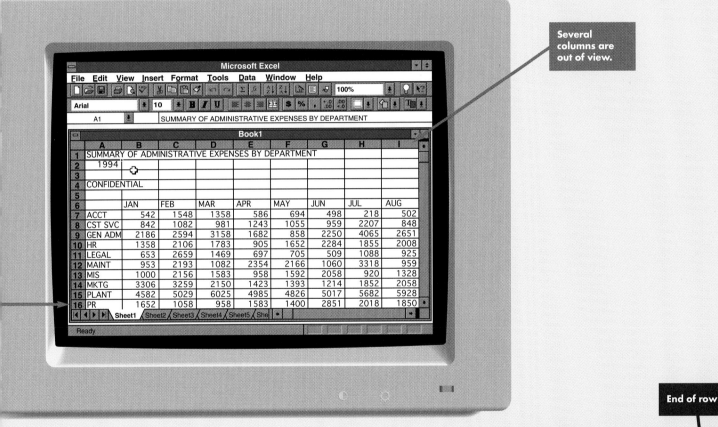

4 To move to the last non-blank cell in the current row, press End and then press Enter.

End of row

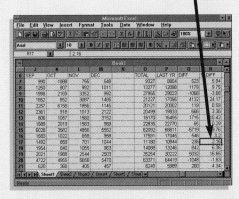

5 To move to a specific cell, first click on Edit in the menu bar and click on the Go To command.

How to Edit Worksheet Contents

There are many reasons to *edit* (change) the contents of a worksheet: to correct a misspelling in a text entry, to revise data, to fix a formula entered incorrectly, and so on. The way you edit cell contents is the same whether the cell contains text, a number, a formula, or a function such as SUM (see Chapter 4).

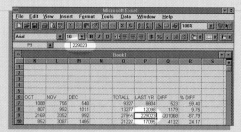

1 Activate the cell you want to edit. To activate a cell, either click on it or move onto it using the arrow keys.

Recalculated formula

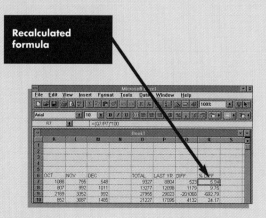

6 Observe that Excel recalculates a formula as soon as you edit it and displays the new result in the cell.

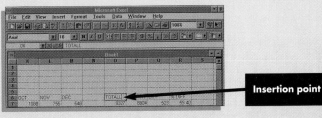

2 To completely replace the cell contents, simply type the new contents and then click on the enter box. It's the same as typing into a blank cell. When you edit data, any formulas or functions relying on that data are recalculated automatically.

3 To modify rather than replace the cell contents, double-click on the cell. A flashing *insertion point* tells you that the cell is ready for editing. If the cell contains formula or function results, the formula or function now appears.

Insertion point

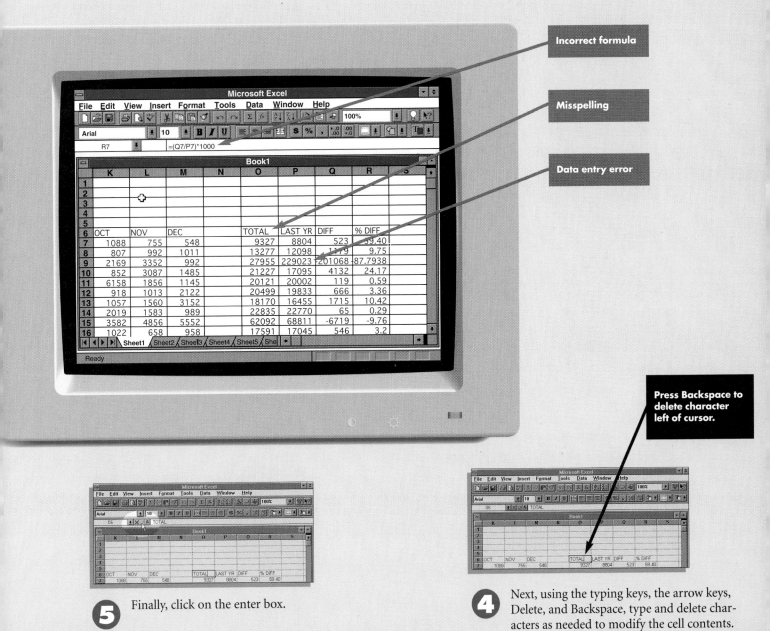

Incorrect formula

Misspelling

Data entry error

Press Backspace to delete character left of cursor.

5 Finally, click on the enter box.

4 Next, using the typing keys, the arrow keys, Delete, and Backspace, type and delete characters as needed to modify the cell contents.

How to Ask "What If?"

What-if analysis is the testing of the impact of sample data. What if the bank reduces the loan rate by one percent? What if our utility bills go up by four thousand dollars next quarter? What if the new salesperson brings in two million dollars in new business next year? What-if analysis in Excel instantly shows you the results of scenarios like these. All you have to do is insert your estimated data in a worksheet and let Excel's automatic recalculation work its magic.

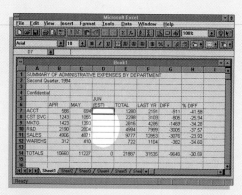

1 Set up an Excel worksheet, leaving room for the data you want to test.

Plug in various possible June results and see how they affect the totals and differences.

		JUN				
		(EST)				
		650				
		1150				
		1400				

APR	MAY	JUN (EST)	TOTAL	LAST YR	DIFF	% DIFF
586	694	650	1930	2191	-261	-11.91
1243	1055	1150	3448	3103	345	11.12
1423	1393	1400	4216	4285	-69	-1.61
2190	2804	2500	7494	7999	-505	-6.31
4906	4871	4890	14667	12853	1814	14.11
312	410	350	1072	1104	-32	-2.90
10660	11227	10940	32827	31535	1292	4.10

② Insert the sample data the same way you insert any data in an Excel worksheet.

③ Observe the results in cells that contain formulas relying on the sample data. You may wish to write down the results or print them (see Chapter 7) so you can compare them with the results obtained from other data estimates.

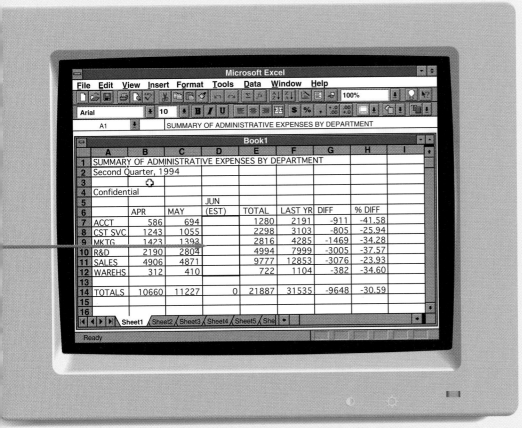

		JUN				
		(EST)				
		800				
		1400				
		1450				
		2500				
		4890				
		350				
		11390				

④ Replace the sample data with new data (as explained on the preceding page).

APR	MAY	JUN (EST)	TOTAL	LAST YR	DIFF	% DIFF
586	694	500	1780	2191	-411	-18.76
1243	1055	900	3198	3103	95	3.06
1423	1393	1350	4166	4285	-119	-2.78
2190	2804	1400	6394	7999	-1605	-20.07
4906	4871	4850	14627	12853	1774	13.80
312	410	210	932	1104	-172	-15.58
10660	11227	9210	31097	31535	-438	-1.39

APR	MAY	JUN (EST)	TOTAL	LAST YR	DIFF	% DIFF
586	694	800	2080	2191	-111	-5.07
1243	1055	1400	3698	3103	595	19.17
1423	1393	1450	4266	4285	-19	-0.44
2190	2804	3500	8494	7999	495	6.19
4906	4871	4950	14727	12853	1874	14.58
312	410	500	1222	1104	118	10.69
10660	11227	12600	34487	31535	2952	9.36

⑥ Repeat steps 4 and 5 until you have tested as many sample values as you need.

⑤ Again observe the results and compare them with the results obtained before.

How to Select a Range

A *range* consists of two or more cells that you define as a group so that you can issue a command affecting all of the cells. Ranges are often made up of rows, columns, or rectangles of adjacent cells, but nonadjacent ranges are common as well. In "How to Sum Numbers" (Chapter 4), you learned how to define a range of adjacent cells in the formula bar by typing the top-left cell, a colon, and the bottom-right cell. In many other cases you will need to define a range not by typing its corner cells but by *selecting* (highlighting) it right on the worksheet. This page shows you how. Future chapters cover the many things you can do to a range once it is selected.

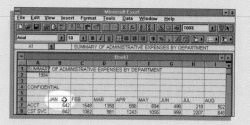

1 Point the mouse pointer to the first cell in the desired range.

Active cell is part of the selection.

TIP SHEET

▶ To select a range from the keyboard, move onto one end or corner of the range using the arrow keys. Then hold down the Shift key, use the arrow keys to move to the opposite end or corner of the range, and release the Shift key. To then add nonadjacent cells to the range, press Shift+F8 to disengage the cell pointer from the current group of cells, move to one end or corner of the next group, press F8 to begin defining the new group, and move to the opposite end or corner. As needed, continue using Shift+F8 and F8 to add more cells to the range.

▶ To unselect a range, click on any cell or press an arrow key. Exception: If you have been selecting a nonadjacent range from the keyboard using Shift+F8 and F8, first press the Escape key; then click on any cell or press an arrow key to unselect the range.

2 Hold down the left mouse button and drag to the opposite end or corner of the range. Cells are selected (highlighted) as you pass over them. Don't worry if part of the range is out of view. Excel will scroll the display when you drag to the edge of the window.

3 Release the mouse button. The cells remain highlighted, defining your range. Skip the remaining steps if one row, column, or rectangle of adjacent cells is all you need.

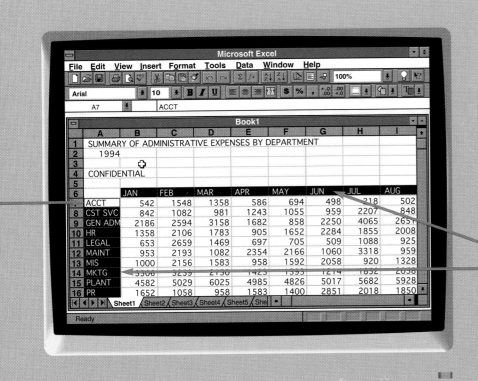

Two nonadjacent groups of cells make up the range.

4 To add other groups of adjacent cells to the range, hold down the Ctrl key. Then drag over the cells as described in steps 1 through 3.

5 To select a single cell as part of a nonadjacent range, hold down Ctrl and click on the cell.

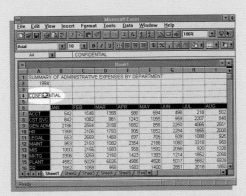

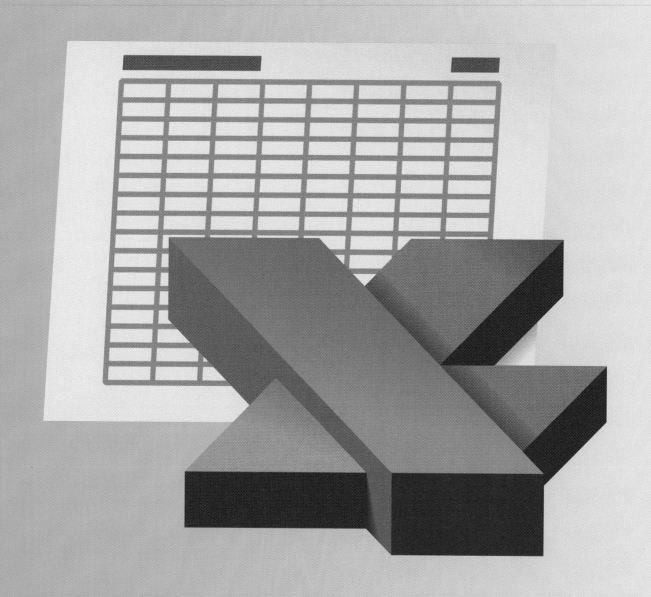

CHAPTER 6

Workbook Access

 Just like the business it supports, a workbook can take on a life of its own. Data are updated, new calculations are required, colleagues request information—a workbook can be with you for months or even years.

Unfortunately, you cannot casually switch off your computer and hope to return to an unsullied workbook later. Computers require special procedures for storing data and returning to it. Follow these procedures and you can safely take a break from your work, confident that your Excel workbooks will be available whenever you want to come back to them.

This chapter covers an array of features collectively called *workbook access*. It explains how to save a workbook, remove it from the screen, and close Excel. It also shows you how to start a new workbook without closing and restarting Excel, how to reopen a saved workbook, and how to use different worksheets within a workbook. These techniques are among the most fundamental you'll learn in this book, and many of the concepts behind them apply to almost any computer program you'll ever use.

How to Save and Close a Workbook

A workbook you are entering on your screen exists only in your computer's memory (RAM), a rather fleeting storage area. RAM is no place to keep something you plan to use later—such as an important or incomplete workbook. If your workbook is even remotely important and if there is any chance that you'll want to come back to it later, you should *save* it on a disk. After saving a workbook, you can continue working on it, or you can close it and then either work on another workbook or exit Excel (see the next three pages).

TIP SHEET

▶ If your computer loses power or other-wise malfunctions, you'll lose whatever is in RAM. On disk, you will still have your workbook exactly as it was last time you saved it—if you saved it at all. After restarting your computer, you can open the workbook from disk and continue working on it. (See "How to Open a Workbook from Disk" later in this chapter.)

▶ If you do not include an extension in your workbook name (see step 2), Excel adds the extension *.XLS* to the name automatically.

▶ Each disk or drive on your computer system is assigned a letter. By convention, drive A refers to the disk in your first (and maybe only) floppy-disk drive. If your computer has two floppy-disk drives, drive B is the lower or rightmost of the two. Drive C is your hard-disk drive. Any drives higher than C are either network drives or additional areas of your hard disk. If you are on a network, check with your network administrator to see what drives you should use.

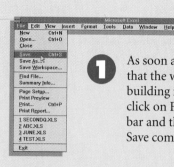

1 As soon as you decide that the workbook you're building is worth saving, click on File in the menu bar and then click on the Save command.

9 If you continue editing your workbook after saving it, your changes will not be saved on disk until you save the workbook again. To do so, click on File in the menu bar and then click on the Save command. Since the workbook already has a name, no dialog box appears. The revised workbook is saved and you can either close the workbook or continue working.

8 Your workbook is now stored safely on disk, but it remains on the screen as well so you can continue working on it. Observe that the document window title bar contains the newly assigned workbook name. If you are done working on this workbook for now, close it by clicking on File in the menu bar and then clicking on the Close command.

2 The Save As dialog box appears. Type a name for the workbook. (The File Name text box is already active, and Excel suggests book1.xls as the name for your first Excel workbook.) A workbook name can contain up to eight characters, followed optionally by a period and an *extension* of up to three characters. The characters ?*."/|[]:|<>+=:, are not permitted in workbook names.

3 Observe the Directories entry in the dialog box. It tells you the disk (drive) and directory where the workbook will be stored if you don't specify otherwise. If this location is okay, skip the next two steps. (A directory is a division of a disk. Usually a directory contains related data and programs. Most hard disks and network disks have directories, but many floppy disks do not.)

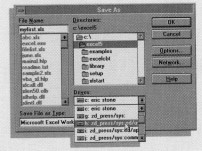

4 To store the workbook on a different disk (drive), click on the arrow to the right of the Drives entry, locate the disk you need (use the scroll bar if necessary) and click on it.

7 If the Summary Info dialog box appears, you can enter information that may later help you remember what the workbook is about. Entering text here is completely optional. When done, click on the OK button.

6 Click on the OK button to save the workbook under the specified name and in the specified location.

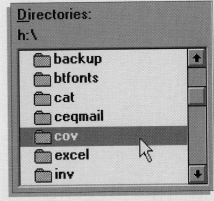

5 To store the workbook in a different directory, locate the directory name in the Directories list (use the scroll bar if necessary) and double-click on it. To see the subdirectories of any directory in the list, double-click on the directory name.

How to Start a New Workbook

Work does not come and go in neat little packets. As you build or edit one workbook, you may be called on to build or access another—pronto. You can start a new workbook anytime Excel is running, even if you have not saved and closed the workbook you are already working on. This page shows you how. Later in the chapter you will learn how to open (redisplay) a workbook you have saved on disk rather than start a new one.

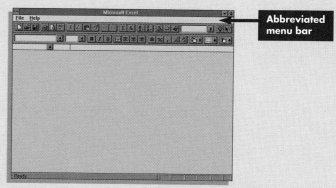

Abbreviated menu bar

1 Observe this abbreviated Excel screen. This screen appears when you have only one workbook open and then you close it (see preceding page). Most of the menu bar is gone because there is no workbook for Excel's commands to operate on. However, the File menu remains so you can start or open a new workbook.

② To start a new workbook, click on File in the menu bar and then click on the New command. (Perform this step whether you have a workbook on your screen or are looking at the abbreviated screen from step 1.)

New title bar

③ Observe the title bar of your new workbook. It may be named Book2, Book3, or even higher. As you start new workbooks throughout a work session, Excel bumps up the number in this temporary name. Of course, this name goes away when you assign a true name to the workbook (see preceding page).

⑤ Remember, other workbooks may remain open—even though you can't see them. To switch back to another open workbook, click on its window if it is visible. Otherwise, click on Window in the menu bar and then click on the workbook name in the bottom part of the menu.

④ Build, edit, save, and close your new workbook.

How to Exit and Restart Excel

I t's wise to shut down Excel when you're done using it. Technically, it is not necessary to close a program before using another one or even before exiting Windows to return to the DOS prompt. However, closing programs you're not using helps your computer run more efficiently. You will also find it easier to use your computer under Windows if the only programs open are the ones you are using or plan to use in the near future.

▶ **You need not exit Excel just to use another Windows program briefly. Press Alt+Esc one or more times to switch among Excel and your other open Windows programs. For example, you can press Alt+Esc to switch to Program Manager, open another program, use it, close it (optional), and press Alt+Esc until you are back in Excel.**

▶ **If you exit Windows without closing Excel and you have left a workbook unsaved, you will be given a chance to save it (see step 4).**

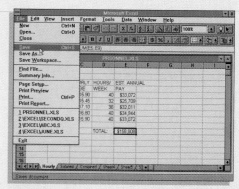

1 Save and close any open workbooks (see preceding pages). Though Excel will remind you to save your workbooks if you forget, taking the initiative to save your work is a good habit to form.

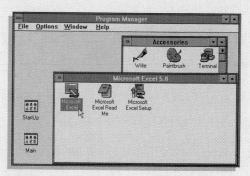

6 Once back in Program Manager, you can restart Excel anytime by opening the program group window containing Excel and double-clicking on its icon (see Chapters 2 and 3).

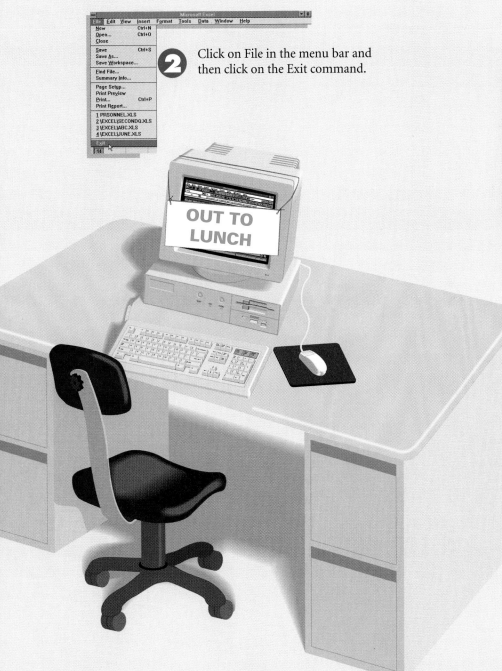

2 Click on File in the menu bar and then click on the Exit command.

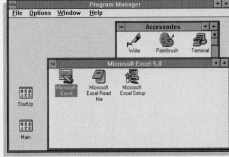

3 If you have no unsaved workbooks, Excel closes and you return immediately to Program Manager.

4 If you have an unsaved workbook or a workbook containing unsaved changes, Excel asks you whether to save it. Click on Yes to save it or on No to abandon it.

5 If you click on Yes and the workbook has never been saved before, the Save As dialog box appears. Name and save the workbook (see "How to Save and Close a Workbook" earlier in this chapter).

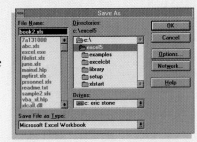

How to Open a Workbook from Disk

The benefit of saving a workbook on disk is that you can later open (redisplay) it for re-examination or revision. You can open a workbook anytime Excel is running. Though Excel imposes no limit on the number of open workbooks, in rare instances you may have so many open workbooks that your computer's memory cannot handle another one. In such a case, Excel warns you of the memory problem and refuses to open the next workbook. Close one or more of your open workbooks and try again.

TIP SHEET

▶ If you open a workbook and change it, be sure to resave it so that your changes are stored on disk. Click on File in the menu bar and then click on the Save command.

▶ Sometimes it's useful to open a workbook, make some changes to it, and save it under a new name. That way you still have the original workbook available on disk under the original name. Click on File in the menu bar and then click on the Save As command. Specify a workbook name and location (see "How to Save and Close a Workbook" at the beginning of this chapter) and click on the OK button. Now your original workbook is stored safely away, and any changes affect the newly named workbook only.

▶ Excel offers a convenient way to open one of the last four workbooks you edited. Click on File in the menu bar and notice the file names at the bottom of the menu. If the workbook you want to open appears on the list, simply click on it.

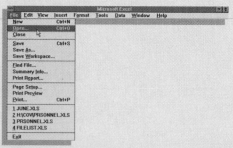

1 Click on File in the menu bar and then click on the Open command.

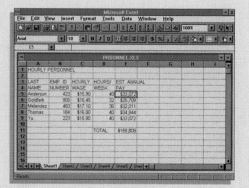

7 The workbook appears on your screen, and its name is in the title bar. You are now free to edit the workbook.

2 In the Open dialog box that appears next, observe the Directories entry. It tells you your computer's *default* drive and directory, the location where it is preset to look for workbooks. If the workbook you want to open is in this location, skip the next two steps.

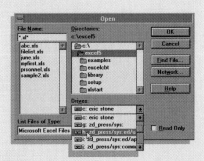

3 If your workbook is on a drive other than the default, click on the arrow to the right of the Drives entry, locate the disk containing the workbook (use the scroll bar if necessary) and click on it. For example, if the workbook is on network drive H, click on drive *h:*.

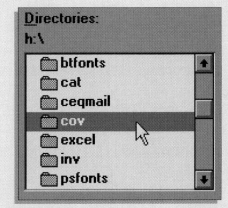

4 If your workbook is on a directory other than the default, locate the directory name in the Directories list (use the scroll bar if necessary) and double-click on it. To see the subdirectories of any directory in the list, double-click on the directory name.

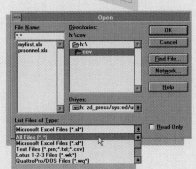

6 In the File Name list, locate the workbook you want to open (use the scroll bar if necessary) and double-click on it.

5 In the File Name list, Excel shows you every file (Excel workbook or other set of data) that is in the specified location and whose name ends with the extension *.XL* followed by any other character. Thus, Excel makes it somewhat easier to open workbooks ending with the standard extension, *.XLS*. To see all files on the directory, click on the arrow to the right of the List Files of Type entry and then click on the first option, All Files (*.*).

How to Work with Worksheets

You may wish to place several related work-sheets (usually called sheets for short) within one workbook. Doing so gives you faster access to your data and lets you easily include a reference to one sheet in another. For example, a personnel workbook might contain one sheet for hourly-wage employees, one sheet for salaried employees, and one sheet combining figures from the two others.

1 To view a new sheet, click on its worksheet tab at the bottom of the workbook window.

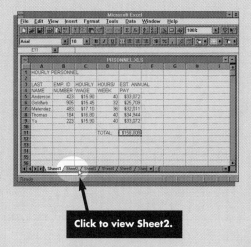

Click to view Sheet2.

▶ You can click on the arrows to the left of the worksheet tabs to scroll different tabs into view. The plain arrows scroll one tab at a time in the direction of the arrow. An arrow with a line scrolls to the last or first tab in the workbook.

▶ As a shortcut, you can display the Rename dialog box (step 3) and rename a sheet by double-clicking on a worksheet tab.

▶ If a sheet name contains special characters such as punctuation marks, you must surround it with apostrophes when using it in a cell or range reference (step 6). For example, if the sheet name were ~abc, you would enter =sum('~abc'!b4:e4) to add the contents of cells B4 through E4 in the ~abc sheet. Note that the closing apostrophe comes before the exclamation point.

"Cell E11 from the Hourly sheet plus cell C9 from the Salaried sheet"

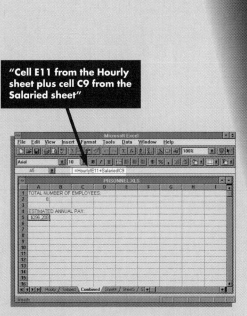

6 In a formula or function, reference a cell or range in another sheet by preceding each cell reference or range with the sheet name followed by an exclamation point (!).

2 Once in a new sheet, you have a clean slate to work with—just like a new page in a paper ledger book. Enter and edit data, formulas, and functions normally as described throughout this book.

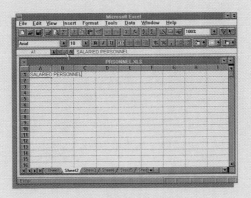

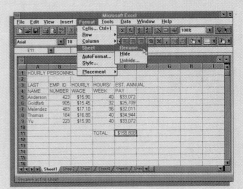

3 Excel starts by naming worksheets Sheet1, Sheet2, and so on, as reflected in the worksheet tabs. It's smart to rename sheets to reflect their content. First, click Format in the menu bar, click on Sheet, and then click on the Rename command.

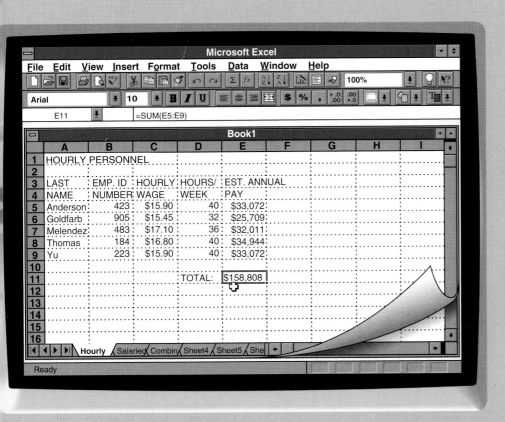

4 Next, in the Rename dialog box, type a name up to 31 characters long for the sheet. The name can include any character.

5 Finally, click on the OK button. The new sheet name will appear on the worksheet tab.

CHAPTER 7

Printing

 The oft-predicted paperless office remains a fantasy. People still rely on printed documents as the primary way to share information.

Excel joins forces with Windows and your printer to provide hassle-free worksheet printing. You can print your entire workbook, the active worksheet, or specific cells—quarterly figures, personnel records of one department, and so on.

Excel is programmed to give you nice-looking printouts. For example, it leaves appropriate margins around the page, and it prints the worksheet name across the top of each page for your reference.

But Excel also lets you customize printouts to your preferences. Let's say your worksheet is so wide that Excel has to print it on two pages. You can tell Excel to print it sideways (*landscape* orientation) rather than the default upright (*portrait* orientation) to try to fit it all on one page. Or tell Excel to squeeze the worksheet onto one page by shrinking the text. One important caveat: The customization options available to you may be limited by the abilities of your printer.

The next page explains how to print all or part of your workbook under Excel's default print settings. The page after that shows you several ways to customize your printouts.

How to Print All or Part of the Worksheet

By default, Excel prints the active worksheet, but you can also have it print the entire workbook or just a selected range of cells. Note that when printing the worksheet or workbook, Excel prints only the rectangle-shaped group of cells whose top-left cell is cell A1 and that is large enough to include every nonblank cell in a worksheet—and no larger. It does not print the usually vast empty spaces at the bottom and right of most worksheets.

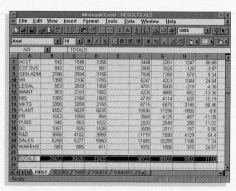

1 If you do not want to print the whole worksheet or workbook, select as a range the cells you want to print. The range can include non-adjacent cells or groups of cells. (See "How to Select a Range" in Chapter 5.)

5 Excel informs you that it is sending your printer a copy of the workbook, worksheet, or selection. If you change your mind about printing the data, click on the Cancel button.

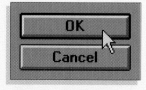

4 Make sure your printer is switched on. Then, in the Print dialog box, click on the OK button.

TIP SHEET

▶ Your printouts may vary from the one shown here if you or another user has already changed the print settings. For example, the gridlines may be absent. See the next page for information on customizing your printouts.

▶ You need not repeat the steps on this page to print multiple copies of your data. Instead, in the Copies text box of the Print dialog box (step 3), type the number of copies you want. Incredibly, you can print up to 32,767 copies at a time. However, if you need more than a few copies, you should consider whether it would be faster and cheaper to print the data once and have it photocopied.

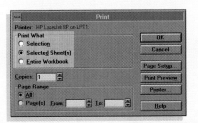

 2 Click on File in the menu bar and then click on the Print command.

3 In the Print dialog box, mark the appropriate radio button: Selection to print the selected cells, Selected Sheet(s) to print the active worksheet (the default), or Entire Workbook.

FIRST

SUMMARY OF ADMINISTRATIVE EXPENSES BY DEPARTMENT							
First Quarter, 1994							
CONFIDENTIAL							
	JAN	FEB	MAR		TOTAL	LAST YR	DIFF	% DIFF
ACCT	542	1548	1358		3448	2201	1247	56.66
CST SVC	842	1082	981		2905	3025	-120	-3.97
GEN ADM	2186	2594	3158		7938	7260	678	9.34
HR	1358	2106	1783		5247	4203	1044	24.84
LEGAL	653	2659	1469		4781	5000	-219	-4.38
MAINT	953	2193	1082		4228	4880	-652	-13.36
MIS	1000	2156	1583		4739	4114	625	15.19
MKTG	3306	3259	2150		8715	5570	3145	56.46
PLANT	4582	5029	6025		15636	17296	-1660	-9.60
PR	1652	1058	958		3668	4125	-457	-11.08
PUBS	845	953	1022		2820	2540	280	11.02
QC	1057	925	1526		3508	3311	197	5.95
R&D	3658	4102	3959		11719	7590	4129	54.40
SALES	6258	5277	5960		17495	16299	1196	7.34
WAREHS	580	885	411		1876	1506	370	24.57
TOTALS	29472	35826	33425		98723	88920	9803	11.02

Page 1

How to Improve Your Printouts

T here are two major ways to improve your printouts. First, you can take steps to fit a wide and/or long worksheet onto one page. And second, you can choose whether to print *cell gridlines* (the lines that separate cells).

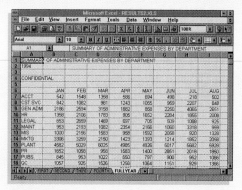

1 Open the workbook and activate the sheet whose print settings you want to change (see Chapter 6).

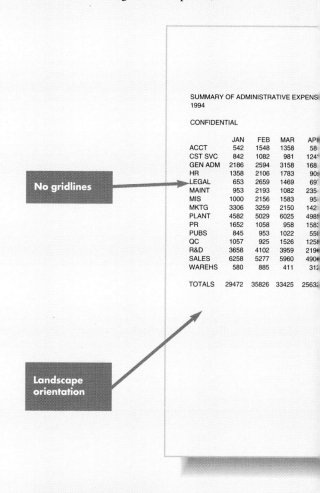

No gridlines

Landscape orientation

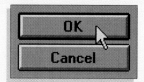

8 When done changing the print settings, click on the OK button.

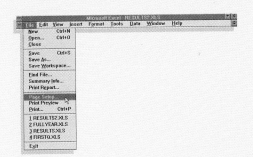

2 Click on File in the menu bar and then click on the Page Setup command.

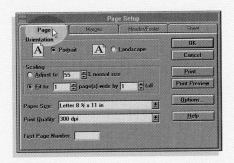

3 At the top of the Page Setup dialog box, click on the Page tab if it is not already active.

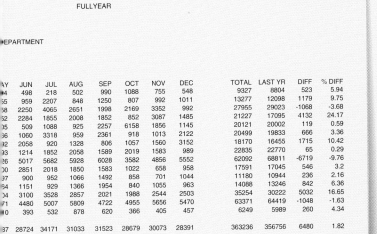

FULLYEAR

EPARTMENT

AY	JUN	JUL	AUG	SEP	OCT	NOV	DEC		TOTAL	LAST YR	DIFF	% DIFF
94	498	218	502	990	1088	755	548		9327	8804	523	5.94
55	959	2207	848	1250	807	992	1011		13277	12098	1179	9.75
58	2250	4065	2651	1998	2169	3352	992		27955	29023	-1068	-3.68
52	2284	1855	2008	1852	852	3087	1485		21227	17095	4132	24.17
05	509	1088	925	2257	6158	1856	1145		20121	20002	119	0.59
36	1060	3318	959	2361	918	1013	2122		20499	19833	666	3.36
92	2058	920	1328	806	1057	1560	3152		18170	16455	1715	10.42
93	1214	1852	2058	1589	2019	1583	989		22835	22770	65	0.29
26	5017	5682	5928	6028	3582	4856	5552		62092	68811	-6719	-9.76
00	2851	2018	1850	1583	1022	658	958		17591	17045	546	3.2
97	900	952	1066	1492	858	701	1044		11180	10944	236	2.16
64	1151	929	1366	1954	840	1055	963		14088	13246	842	6.36
04	3100	3528	2857	2021	1988	2544	2503		35254	30222	5032	16.65
71	4480	5007	5809	4722	4955	5656	5470		63371	64419	-1048	-1.63
0	393	532	878	620	366	405	457		6249	5989	260	4.34
37	28724	34171	31033	31523	28679	30073	28391		363236	356756	6480	1.82

4 If you wish, change the orientation by clicking on the Landscape or Portrait radio button. Switching to landscape (sideways) orientation is often all it takes to fit a wide sheet onto one page.

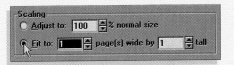

5 To shrink the text just enough to fit each sheet on one page, click in the Fit To radio button.

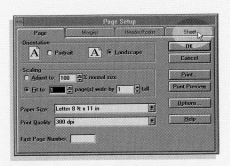

6 If you want to specify whether gridlines should be printed, first click on the Sheet tab.

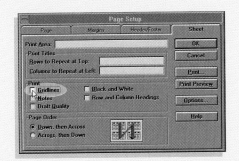

7 Next, clear the Gridlines check box to omit gridlines, or mark this check box to include them.

TRY IT!

Here is an opportunity to try out the many Excel skills you've acquired in the first seven chapters of this book. Follow these steps to build, edit, and print the worksheet pictured here. For many steps, chapter numbers are included to help you find more information on the skills required. In upcoming chapters, you'll learn about certain techniques that would make this sheet more readable. For example, you will learn how to align the column headings over the numbers below them and how to express the % DIFF figures in fewer decimal places.

With Excel running, click on File in the menu bar and then click on the New command. You will start a new worksheet, although this is necessary only if you already have a worksheet on your screen. *Chapter 6*

File	
New	Ctrl+N
Open...	Ctrl+O
Close	
Save	Ctrl+S
Save As...	
Save Workspace...	
Find File...	
Summary Info...	
Page Setup...	
Print Preview	
Print...	Ctrl+P
Print Report...	
1 TEST.XLS	
2 SECONDQ.XLS	
3 ABC.XLS	
4 JUNE.XLS	
Exit	

FIRSTQ

REVENUES BY CATEGORY, IN THOUSANDS								
First Quarter, 1994								
CORP	JAN							
DIR MAIL	366	FEB	MAR					
MISC DIR	330	410	396		TOTAL	LAST YR	DIFF	% DIFF
PROMO	58	325	215		1172	1259	-87	-6.91025
RETAIL	54	88	41		870	777	93	11.96911
	626	154	135		187	210	-23	-10.9524
TOTAL		527	596		343	320	23	7.1875
	1434	1504	1383		1749	1630	119	7.300613
					4321	4196	125	2.979028

2

Press the Caps Lock key to type in all uppercase, and in cell A1 type REV-ENUES BY CATEGORY, IN THOUSANDS.

3

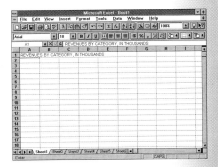

Click on the enter box to enter the cell contents you just typed. *Chapter 4*

4

A2			1q, 1994	
	A	B	C	D	E
1	REVENUES BY CATEGORY, IN THOUSANDS				
2	1q, 1994				
3					

Click in cell A2 to activate it, press Caps Lock to switch back to normal typing, type **1q, 1994** (short for *First Quarter, 1994*) and click on the enter box. *Chapter 4*

5

Enter all of the remaining column and row headings as shown here and in the printout to the left.

6

		JAN	FEB	MAR
4		JAN	FEB	MAR
5	CORP	366	410	396
6	DIR MAIL	330	325	215
7	MISC DIR	58	88	41
8	PROMO	54	154	135
9	RETAIL	626	527	596

Enter the January, February, and March data for each of the five categories as shown here.

7

B11			=sum(b5:b9)	
	A	B	C	D	E
1	REVENUES BY CATEGORY, IN THOUSANDS				
2	1q, 1994				
3					
4		JAN	FEB	MAR	
5	CORP	366	410	396	
6	DIR MAIL	330	325	215	
7	MISC DIR	58	88	41	
8	PROMO	54	154	135	
9	RETAIL	626	527	596	
10					
11	TOTAL	=sum(b5:b9)			

In cell B11, type =**sum(b5:b9)** and click on the enter box. This function sums the five numbers above cell B11. *Chapter 4*

8

D11			=SUM(D5:D9)	
	A	B	C	D	E
1	REVENUES BY CATEGORY, IN THOUSANDS				
2	1q, 1994				
3					
4		JAN	FEB	MAR	
5	CORP	366	410	396	
6	DIR MAIL	330	325	215	
7	MISC DIR	58	88	41	
8	PROMO	54	154	135	
9	RETAIL	626	527	596	
10					
11	TOTAL	1434	1504	1383	

In cell C11, enter a function to sum the February data, and in cell D11, enter a function to sum the March data. (Hint: Use the SUM function as in step 8 but with different cell ranges.)

9

F5			=sum(b5:d5)			
	A	B	C	D	E	F	G
1	REVENUES BY CATEGORY, IN THOUSANDS						
2	1q, 1994						
3							
4		JAN	FEB	MAR		TOTAL	LAST YR
5	CORP	366	410	396		=sum(b5:d5)	
6	DIR MAIL	330	325	215			
7	MISC DIR	58	88	41			
8	PROMO	54	154	135			
9	RETAIL	626	527	596			
10							
11	TOTAL	1434	1504	1383			

In cell F5, enter =**sum(b5:d5)** to add the totals for corporate revenues in row 5. *Chapter 4*

10

F9			=SUM(B9:D9)		
	A	B	C	D	E	F
1	REVENUES BY CATEGORY, IN THOUSANDS					
2	1q, 1994					
3						
4		JAN	FEB	MAR		TOTAL
5	CORP	366	410	396		1172
6	DIR MAIL	330	325	215		870
7	MISC DIR	58	88	41		187
8	PROMO	54	154	135		343
9	RETAIL	626	527	596		1749
10						
11	TOTAL	1434	1504	1383		4321

Using the SUM function as in step 10 but with different cell ranges, fill in the rest of the TOTAL column. For example, in cell F6 enter =**sum(b6:d6)**. In cell F11, enter =**sum(b11:d11)** to get a grand total by summing the sums calculated in row 11.

Continue to next page ▶

TRY IT!

Continue
below

11

Enter the
data as
shown for
the LAST YR
column.
These num-
bers (includ-

<table>
<tr><td>LAST YR</td></tr>
<tr><td>1259</td></tr>
<tr><td>777</td></tr>
<tr><td>210</td></tr>
<tr><td>320</td></tr>
<tr><td>1630</td></tr>
<tr><td>4196</td></tr>
</table>

ing the total in cell G11) are plain data,
not formula results.

12

In cell H5,
enter the for-
mula =**f5-g5**
to subtract
last year's
first-quarter revenues from this year's.
Then, in cells H6 through H9 and cell
H11, enter similar formulas, adjusting
only the cell references. For example,
the formula in cell H6 should be
=**F6-G6.** *Chapter 4*

13

In cell I5,
enter the
formula
=**h5/g5** and
observe the
result, –0.0691. This formula expresses
the difference between last year's
quarterly revenues in the Corporate
category and this year's as a proportion
of last year's quarterly Corporate
revenues. You need to multiply this
number by 100 to get a percent figure.

14

<table>
<tr><td>% DIFF</td></tr>
<tr><td>=H5/G5</td></tr>
</table>

Double-click
on cell I5 to activate the formula for
editing and place the insertion point at
the end of the formula. *Chapter 5*

15

Type *****100**
and click on
the enter box.
Notice that
cell I5 now
shows the correct percent figure.
Chapter 5

16

Enter similar
formulas
(with appro-
priate cell
references) in
cells I6 through I9 and cell I11.

17

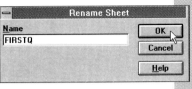

Click on cell
A2, type **First Quarter, 1994** and click
on the enter box to edit this cell.
Chapter 5

22

Type **FIRSTQ**
(all upper-
case) to give
the sheet a new name which will appear on printouts of the sheet. Then
click on the OK button. *Chapter 6*

18

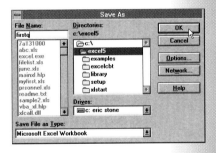

Click on File
in the menu
bar and then
click on the
Save
command.
Chapter 6

23

Click on File
in the menu
bar and then
click on the
Print
command.
Chapter 7

19

Type **firstq** in
the File Name
text box of
the Save As
dialog box.
Then click on
the OK but-
ton to save the workbook under the name
FIRSTQ.XLS. *Chapter 6*

24

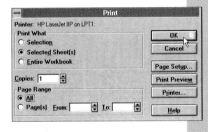

In the Print
dialog box,
click on the
OK button to
print one
copy of the
worksheet. *Chapter 7*

20

If the
Summary
Info dialog
box appears,
click on the
OK button.

25

Click on File
in the menu
bar and then
click on the
Close com-
mand to close
the work-
book. When
asked
whether you
want to save
the workbook, click on the Yes button.
Chapter 6

21

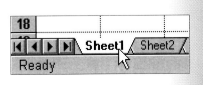

Double-click
on the Sheet1
worksheet tab. *Chapter 6*

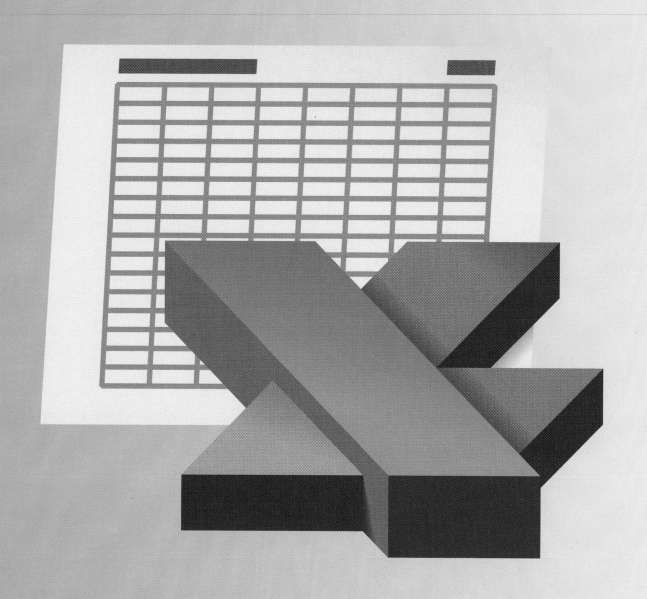

CHAPTER 8

Changing Worksheet Structure

 As your business evolves, so do your Excel worksheets. What happens to your personnel worksheets when employees come and go? What about when the accounting department tells you that the numbers you budgeted to one category belong under another?

Changes like these require more than the cell editing you learned in Chapter 5. They require you to restructure your worksheets. Worksheet restructuring was a major headache in the days of ledger books. With Excel, it's a real breeze.

This chapter covers the most important types of worksheet restructuring. You'll learn how to accommodate new data by adding columns and rows to a sheet. You'll learn how to delete cells and cell contents—including entire columns and rows. You'll discover how to "drag" data with the mouse from one part of a sheet to another. And you'll see how to adjust the width of a column so that it displays all the data inside it without wasting space.

How to Insert Columns and Rows

To add new data to a worksheet, you have to make room for it. Let's say you have a personnel sheet whose rows are arranged in alphabetical order by the employee's last name. When a new employee joins the company, you must add this person not at the bottom of the sheet but in the proper alphabetical location. To do this, you add a blank row to the sheet and insert the new data.

TIP SHEET

▶ There's an alternative to adding rows of data in certain places just to maintain alphabetical order or another sequencing scheme. Instead, add the rows anywhere—maybe below all the existing rows—and later sort the data using Excel's powerful Sort command. See Chapter 14.

▶ When you insert rows or columns, data below or to the right of the insertion shifts. What happens to formulas and functions containing references to the shifted data? Excel corrects them automatically. For example, in step 5 you can see that Charles Lambert's vacation record, formerly in row 6, is now in row 7. Cell H6 used to contain =SUM(D6:G6). Now that Lambert's record has shifted down, his balance, now in cell H7, is obtained by the function =SUM(D7:G7).

▶ Data you add within the range of an existing formula or function are calculated in the formula or function. For example, if your worksheet contained the function =SUM(D4:D8) and you added a row of data above row 6, the data in the new row would become part of the calculation, which now reads =SUM (D4:D9). However, data added outside the range of a formula or function are not calculated in that formula or function—a situation that you may need to remedy. Using the same example, if you add a new row below row 8 and you want the new data to be part of the SUM function, you must edit the function to read =SUM(D4:D9).

Insert one row above row 6.

1 If you want to insert one row, activate any cell in the row immediately below the place where you want to insert it. To insert multiple rows, indicate the number of rows to insert by selecting at least one cell in the same number of rows, starting in the row immediately below the desired insertion point. For example, to insert three rows above row 5, select at least one cell in each of rows 5, 6, and 7.

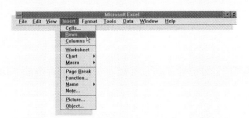

2 Then, to insert one or more rows as indicated in step 1, click on Insert in the menu bar and then click on the Rows command.

Insert two columns to the left of column H.

3 If you want to insert one column, activate any cell in the column immediately to the right of the place where you want to insert it. To insert multiple columns, indicate the number of columns to insert by selecting at least one cell in the same number of columns, starting in the column immediately to the right of the desired insertion point. For example, to insert three columns to the left of column D, select at least one cell in each of columns D, E, and F.

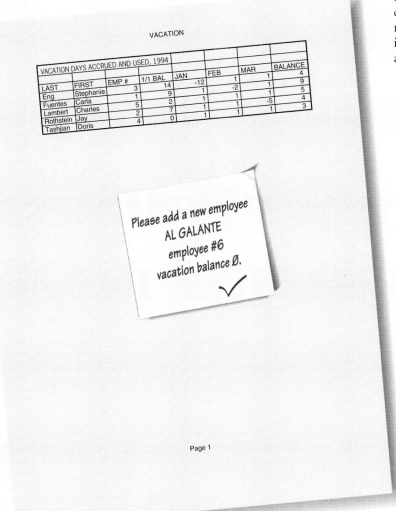

4 Then, to insert one or more columns as indicated in step 3, click on Insert in the menu bar and then click on the Columns command.

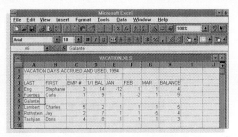

5 Add data to the new rows or columns normally.

How to Delete or Clear Cells

To *delete* a cell is to remove the cell from the worksheet, closing up the vacated space by shifting either the cells on the right or the cells below. To *clear* a cell is to delete its contents and leave an empty cell. Often, you delete an entire row or column. For example, in a personnel worksheet, you might delete the row containing the record of an employee who left the company. On the other hand, you may need to clear any number of cells—even non-adjacent ones—when you know the data they contain are wrong or outdated but you do not yet know what to put in their place.

Column, row, or cell to delete

1 To delete one row or one column, activate any cell in the row or column. To delete multiple adjacent rows or columns, select at least one cell in each one. To delete specific cells but not entire rows or columns, select those cells. (Skip to step 5 if you want to clear cells rather than delete them.)

TIP SHEET

▶ **When you delete cells, data below or to the right of the deletion shifts. However, Excel automatically adjusts formulas and functions that reference the shifted data so that they continue to produce the original result.**

▶ **When you need to replace data, there's no point clearing the cell and then entering the new data. Simply activate the cell and enter the new data, which replaces the old data automatically.**

▶ **Observe this quirk of Excel terminology: The Delete key *clears* cell contents; it does not *delete* cells from the worksheet. Thus, pressing the Delete key (step 6) is not the same as issuing the Delete command from the edit menu (step 2).**

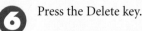

6 Press the Delete key.

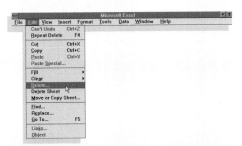

2 Click on Edit in the menu bar and then click on the Delete command.

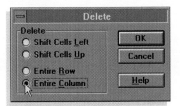

3 In the Delete dialog box, mark the Entire Row radio button to delete one or more adjacent rows; or mark the Entire Column radio button to delete one or more adjacent columns; or, to delete only the selected cells, mark the proper radio button to reflect how you want the vacated space filled: Shift Cells Up or Shift Cells Left.

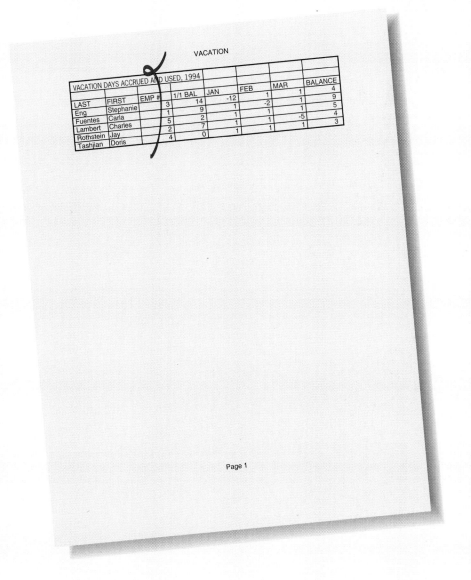

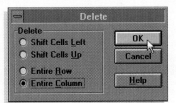

4 Click on the OK button. (Skip the remaining steps unless you want to clear cells rather than delete them.)

Cells to clear

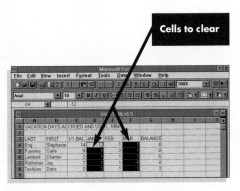

5 To clear cells, select them. (They need not be adjacent cells.) Or, to clear one cell, simply activate it.

How to Move and Copy Data

Excel's "drag-and-drop" editing feature is one of the most intuitive operations in all of computerdom. It lets you move or copy data by dragging it into place with the mouse much as you might scoop something up and reposition it with your bare hands. Beware that drag-and-drop editing can delete data unless you specify otherwise (see step 7).

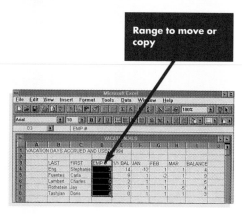

Range to move or copy

1 Activate the cell or select the range of cells you want to move or copy.

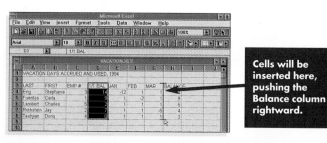

Cells will be inserted here, pushing the Balance column rightward.

7 To avoid overwriting nonblank cells in a move or copy operation, hold down the Shift key before releasing the mouse button in step 4 or 5. When you hold down the Shift key, the outline changes to a vertical or horizontal I-beam, indicating where the cells will be inserted and whether other cells will be pushed to the right (vertical I-beam) or downward (horizontal) to accommodate the insertion.

Replace contents of destination cells?

6 If you are moving the cell(s) and you drop them into an occupied area of the worksheet, Excel asks you whether you want to overwrite the nonblank cells, deleting their previous contents. Click on the OK button if you do; otherwise, click on the Cancel button to cancel the operation. (See the next step to learn how to move or copy cells without overwriting data—and beware that you get no warning about overwriting cells when you are copying rather than moving data.)

TIP SHEET

▶ In a standard move operation (step 4), the vacated cells are cleared, not deleted. This means that empty cells remain in your worksheet. See the preceding page if you want to delete the empty cells.

▶ When you move cells, formulas and functions that refer to these cells individually are updated to reflect the new cell location. Thus, formula results do not change. However, cell ranges (two cells separated by a colon) in functions such as SUM are updated only if you move the entire range of cells specified in the function. When you move individual cells from within the range, the function is not updated. If your worksheet has SUM functions (or other functions—see Chapter 10) containing cell ranges, recheck them carefully after moving data, and edit them if necessary.

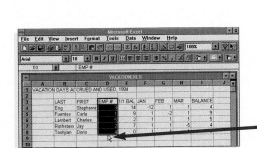

Destination

Mouse pointer

2 Point to the border of the cell or range so that the mouse pointer changes from a cross to an arrow.

3 Hold down the left mouse button and drag to the desired spot. An outline shows you where the cell(s) you are moving or copying will be inserted if you release the mouse button at that moment.

VACATION

VACATION DAYS ACCRUED AND USED, 1994								
EMP #	LAST	FIRST	EMP #	1/1 BAL	JAN	FEB	MAR	BALANCE
3	Eng	Stephanie	3	14	-12	1	1	4
1	Fuentes	Carla	1	9	1	-2	1	9
5	Lambert	Charles	5	2	1	1	1	5
2	Rothstein	Jay	2	7	1	1	-5	4
4	Tashjian	Doris	4	0	1	1	1	3

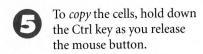

DRAG & DROP

5 To *copy* the cells, hold down the Ctrl key as you release the mouse button.

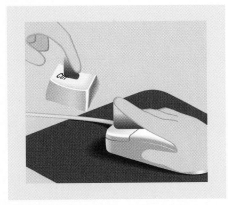

4 To *move* the cell(s), simply release the mouse button.

How to Adjust Column Width

Excel's default column width is often inadequate to display long headings, large numbers, and numbers taken to many decimal places. When a column is not wide enough to display its content, Excel truncates the content (for text when the cell to the right is occupied, or for numbers with many decimal places) or, for large numbers, expresses it either in scientific notation or as *overflow markers* (######). However, Excel "remembers" the complete content of the cell, displaying it in the formula bar when the cell is active, and using it when the cell is referenced in a formula or function. To display the complete content in the cell, you can widen the column. Through the same technique, you can narrow a space-wasting column so that it is no wider than necessary to display its content.

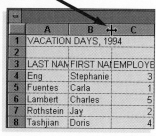

Mouse pointer

1 In the column you want to widen or narrow, point to the line to the right of the column heading. Notice the shape of the mouse pointer.

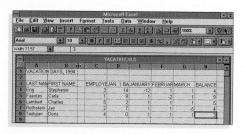

4 As necessary, repeat steps 1 through 3 to further refine the column width and to adjust other columns.

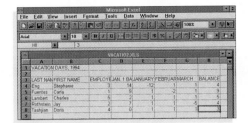

2 Hold down the left mouse button and drag the mouse to the right (to widen the column) or to the left (to narrow it).

3 Release the mouse button and observe the data within the column to determine whether the column has reached its optimal width. Are data truncated unnecessarily? Or, on the other hand, is space wasted?

VACATION

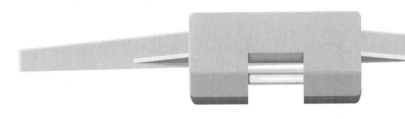

VACATION DAYS, 1994							
LAST NAME	FIRST NAME	EMPLOYEE #	JAN. 1 BALANCE	JANUARY	FEBRUARY	MARCH	BALANCE
Eng	Stephanie	3	14	-12		1	4
Fuentes	Carla	1	9	1	-2	1	9
Lambert	Charles	5	2	1	1	1	5
Rothstein	Jay	2	7	1	1	-5	4
Tashjian	Doris	4	0	1	1	1	3

CHAPTER 9

Improving Worksheet Appearance

 You build a worksheet mainly for accuracy and usability, but there's room for aesthetics, too. Text enhancements such as boldface can draw the eyes toward important information. Rounding numbers off to a reasonable number of decimal places can help you and your readers to put data into perspective. And from a purely cynical standpoint, a nice-looking worksheet can enhance the impact of good news and soften the blow of bad news.

Excel offers a variety of formatting features that can improve the appearance of your worksheets both on the screen and in print. In this chapter, you will learn how to format text and numbers, how to enhance cells by applying shading and special border lines, how to change the alignment of cell contents within the cell borders, and how to center a long heading over the cells below it.

Excel makes it pretty easy to apply sophisticated formatting to your worksheets. Don't let this ease tempt you into excessive formatting. An overly stylized worksheet wastes your time, masks information, and impresses no one. Apply formatting judiciously and you'll find it far more effective.

How to Format Text

The major text formatting choices in Excel are font (typeface, such as Courier and Times Roman), font style (boldface and italics), and size (measured in points, where 72 points equal about 1 inch). To format text in Excel you actually format a cell. Whatever happens to be in the cell takes on the assigned format. The formatting remains in effect as you edit the cell content. You can format a cell even when it is blank; later, when you insert text, a number, or a formula result in the cell, the new content takes on the assigned format.

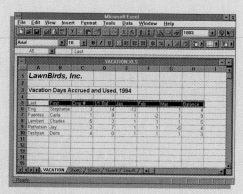

1 Activate the cell you want to format, or select a range of cells to format all of them the same.

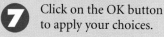

7 Click on the OK button to apply your choices.

2 Click on Format in the menu bar and then click on the Cells command.

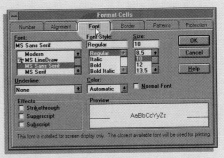

3 At the top of the Format Cells dialog box, click on the Font tab if it is not already active.

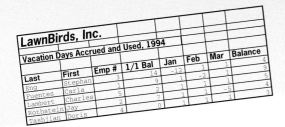

4 To change the font (typeface), locate the desired font name in the Font list and click on it. (You may need to scroll the Font list to display the font you need.)

5 To change the font style, locate the style you need in the Font Style list—you may need to use the scroll bar—and click on it.

6 To change the type size, locate the desired size in the Size list—again, you may need to scroll—and click on it.

How to Format Numbers

Excel follows certain default rules for the display of numbers in worksheet cells. For example, a minus sign denotes a negative number, and there are no commas to separate thousands (unless you entered the number with commas). However, this is merely Excel's General number format. You are free to choose from a wide array of number formats for any cell. For example, you can format a cell containing a dollar amount to include the dollar sign, to express no decimal places (rounding numbers to the nearest dollar), and to display negative numbers in red and in parentheses. Number formatting affects only the display of numbers within worksheet cells. The complete number, formula, or function appears in the formula bar when the cell is active, and even when a number is truncated and rounded off for display, the complete number is used in calculations.

▶ **To go back to Excel's default number format, follow the same steps given here. In step 4, select All from the Category list. In step 5, select General from the Format Codes list.**

▶ **If a cell is formatted with the default General format but you enter a number with a dollar sign or % symbol, Excel automatically assigns the cell a Currency or Percentage format.**

▶ **The Percentage format multiplies a number by 100 and adds a percent sign. Therefore, you should enter numbers into Percentage-formatted cells as decimals. For example, to have a Percentage-formatted cell display 35%, enter .35. If you enter 35, the cell will display 3500%.**

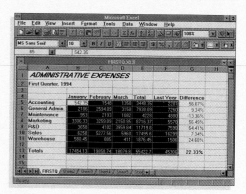

1 Activate the cell whose number format you want to change, or select a range of cells to assign the same number format to all of them.

8 Click on the OK button.

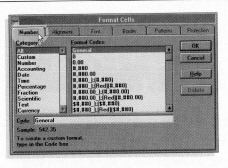

2 Click on Format in the menu bar and then click on the Cells command.

3 At the top of the Format Cells dialog box, click on the Number tab if it is not already active.

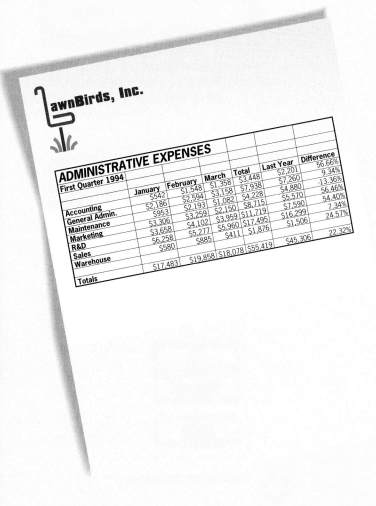

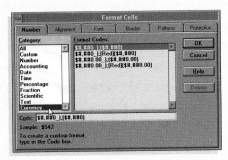

4 In the Category list, click on the category that best describes the type of number you have put or plan to put in the cell(s). For example, click on Currency if you are working with dollar figures. When you select Currency, Excel narrows the number formats in the Format Codes list to those appropriate for dollar amounts. To see a list of all the available number formats, select All in the Category list.

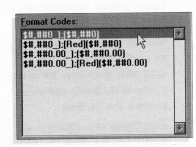

5 In the Format Codes list, click on a number format. In Excel's format codes, a zero means that a place will always be occupied, even by an unnecessary zero. For example, the 0.00 Number format displays .3 as 0.30.

7 A semicolon in a format code separates the treatment of positive numbers from the treatment of negative numbers. Notice, for example, that all Currency formats place negative numbers in parentheses and that some of them display negative numbers in red as well.

6 A pound sign (#) in a format code prevents unnecessary zeros but shows what will happen if the indicated digits are present. For example, the #,##0 Number format displays 1432 as 1,432, but displays 55 simply as 55.

How to Format Cells

Cell borders and cell shading are excellent
ways to highlight important worksheet information and to improve general worksheet
appearance, both on the screen and in print.
Like all formatting, cell formatting should be
applied sparingly lest it lose its impact.
Common uses of cell formatting include shading column headings and adding a thick border
to a cell that shows a grand total. When working with ranges of adjacent cells, you have a
choice of placing a border around the entire
range or along the edges of each selected cell.

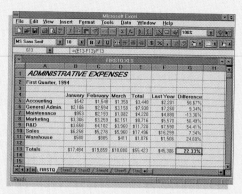

1 Activate the cell you want to
format, or select a range of
cells to format all of them.

9 Click on the OK button.

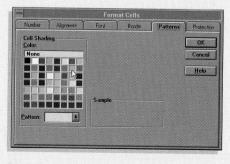

8 Click on the desired shading color.

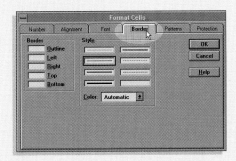

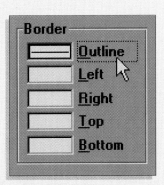

2 Click on Format in the menu bar and then click on the Cells command.

3 In the Format Cells dialog box, click on the Border tab if it is not already active.

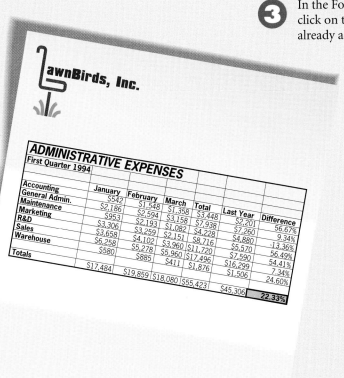

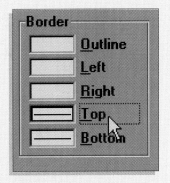

4 To add a border around the active cell or around the group of selected cells, click on Outline.

5 To place a border along just certain sides of the cell or of each selected cell, click on the appropriate option(s): Left, Right, Top, and/or Bottom. To place a complete border around every cell in the selected range, click on all four of these options.

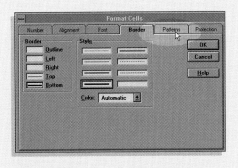

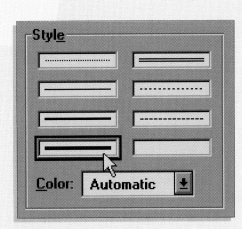

7 If you want to shade the cell(s), click on the Patterns tab.

6 Click on the desired border style.

How to Align Cell Contents

By default, Excel right-aligns numbers, including formula results, within the cell borders, and left-aligns text. Excel calls this alignment scheme the General option. Sometimes the General alignment is inadequate. It is especially problematic when left-aligned column headings (text) are atop columns of right-aligned numbers. However, Excel makes it easy to change the way cell contents align with cell borders. When you change alignment, you technically are formatting the cell, not the cell content. Therefore, if you later edit the cell content, the alignment remains in effect.

TIP SHEET

▶ **To go back to default alignment (right-aligned numbers, left-aligned text), follow the same steps given on this page, but in step 3 click on General.**

▶ **Sometimes numbers are used not as data but as *labels* (nondata cell contents such as column and row headings). For example, in a worksheet comparing yearly results, each of several years (1993, 1994, 1995, ...) might be a column heading. However, Excel will right-align such labels (just as it right-aligns all numbers by default) unless you specifically tell Excel that the number is a label. To do so, type an apostrophe before the number. For example, enter '1994 in a cell to display 1994 and have Excel treat it as text for default alignment purposes.**

▶ **You cannot achieve decimal alignment of a column of numbers through the procedure described on this page. Instead, simply select for the cells any number format that allows a specific number of decimal places.**

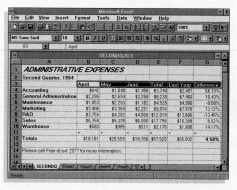

1 Activate the cell whose alignment you want to change, or select a range of cells to specify the same alignment for all of them.

8 Click on the OK button.

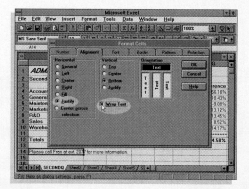

7 Click on the Wrap Text check box to cause wide text entries to break into separate lines within the cell, increasing the row height, rather than spill into the cell(s) to the right. Then, optionally, click on the Justify radio button to *justify* lines within the cell, causing Excel to add space between words as necessary so that lines are both right- and left-aligned between the cell borders.

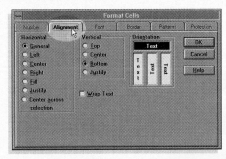

② Click on Format in the menu bar and then click on the Cells command.

③ At the top of the Format Cells dialog box, click on the Alignment tab if it is not already active.

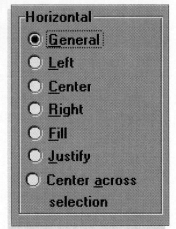

awnBirds, Inc.

ADMINISTRATIVE EXPENSES

Second Quarter, 1994

	April	May	June	Total	Last Year	Difference
Accounting	$642	$1,648	$1,458	$3,748	$2,401	56.10%
General Administration	$2,286	$2,694	$3,258	$8,238	$7,460	10.43%
Maintenance	$1,053	$2,293	$1,182	$4,528	$4,980	-9.08%
Marketing	$3,406	$3,359	$2,251	$9,016	$7,970	13.12%
R&D	$3,756	$4,202	$4,060	$12,018	$13,886	-13.45%
Sales	$6,358	$5,378	$6,060	$17,796	$16,399	8.52%
Warehouse	$680	$985	$511	$2,176	$1,906	14.17%
Totals	$18,181	$20,559	$18,780	$57,520	$55,002	4.58%

Please call Fran at ext.
2077 for more information.

④ In the Horizontal area of the Format dialog box, click on the radio button reflecting the alignment you want, as described in the next three steps. (The Center across Selection option is described on the next page.)

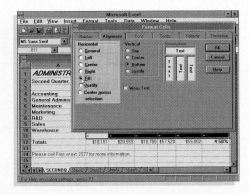

⑥ The Fill option repeats the cell contents until the cell is full. This option is useful mainly for decorative touches such as filling a row of cells with dashes or, as in the worksheet on this page, with equal signs.

⑤ The Left, Center, and Right radio buttons produce, respectively, alignment with the left cell border, centering between the cell borders, and alignment with the right cell border.

How to Center a Heading over Multiple Columns

A major heading in a worksheet may look better when centered over the entire worksheet or over the columns to which it refers. Excel helps you achieve this effect in just a few steps.

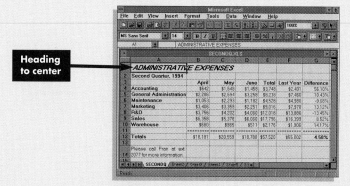

Heading to center

1 Enter the heading in column A or in the leftmost column of the group over which the heading is to be centered.

6 Click on the OK button.

2 Select the heading and, to its right, all the columns over which to center the heading.

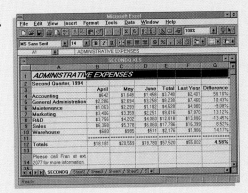

3 Click on Format in the menu bar and then click on the Cells command.

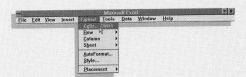

4 At the top of the Format Cells dialog box, click on the Alignment tab if it is not already active.

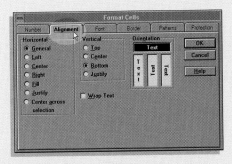

ADMINISTRATIVE EXPENSES

Second Quarter, 1994

	April	May	June	Total	Last Year	Difference
Accounting	$642	$1,648	$1,458	$3,748	$2,401	56.10%
General Administration	$2,286	$2,694	$3,258	$8,238	$7,460	10.43%
Maintenance	$1,053	$2,293	$1,182	$4,528	$4,980	-9.08%
Marketing	$3,406	$3,359	$2,251	$9,016	$7,970	13.12%
R&D	$3,756	$4,202	$4,060	$12,018	$13,886	-13.45%
Sales	$6,358	$5,378	$6,060	$17,796	$16,399	8.52%
Warehouse	$680	$985	$511	$2,176	$1,906	14.17%
Totals	$18,181	$20,559	$18,780	$57,520	$55,002	**4.58%**

Please call Fran at ext.
2077 for more information.

5 Click on the Center across Selection radio button.

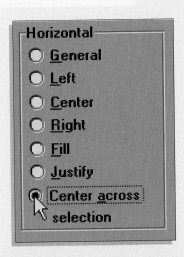

Horizontal

- ○ **G**eneral
- ○ **L**eft
- ○ **C**enter
- ○ **R**ight
- ○ **F**ill
- ○ **J**ustify
- ● Center across selection

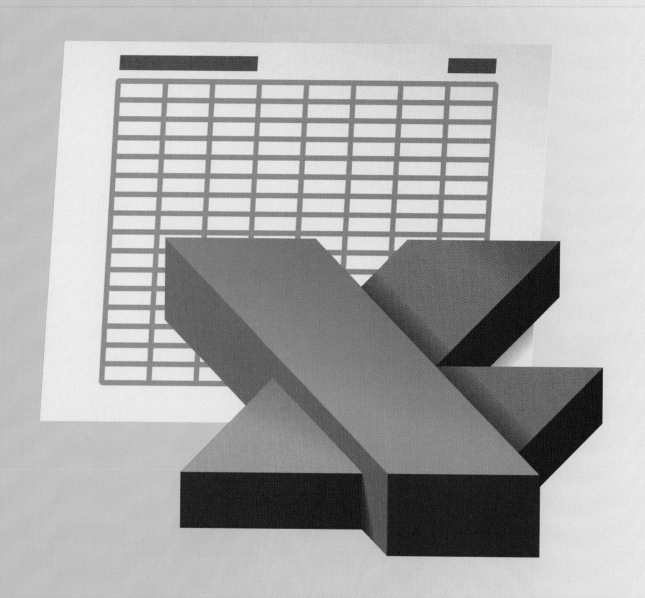

CHAPTER 10

Adding Worksheet Capabilities

Excel comes with a vast array of tools designed to make your worksheets easier to build and more functional. Some of these tools are so specialized that you might use Excel day in and day out for years and never need them. Yet for other people these same tools are indispensable.

This chapter covers a few tools that *no* Excel user should be without. You will learn more about Excel's functions, which perform operations that would be inconvenient or impossible to perform with ordinary formulas. You will learn a great way to build worksheets faster by "filling in" repetitive formulas or functions—and letting Excel figure out the correct cell references! This technique spares you from typing the formulas or functions from scratch. And in this chapter you will even learn how to override Excel's automatic adjustment of cell references when necessary.

How to Use Excel's Functions

This page presents three of Excel's most useful functions: MAX, MIN, and AVERAGE. Chapter 4 explained that a *function* is like a built-in formula. For example, the SUM function is a way to sum the contents of several cells without building a long formula to add each one. Excel offers many functions, and not all of them are mere conveniences like SUM. Certain Excel functions perform actions that do not duplicate standard formulas. For instance, the MAX function displays the largest (maximum) value of a range you specify. No formula could do that for you.

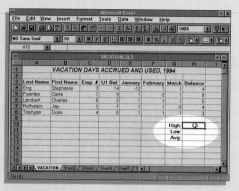

1 Activate the cell where you want the function result to appear.

TIP SHEET

▶ To include noncontiguous ranges or individual cells in any function, separate the ranges or cell references with commas, as in =min(b4:d8,f4:g8,i10,j10).

▶ By convention, function names are written in uppercase, but when typing them in Excel, you can use uppercase, lowercase, or a combination of the two.

▶ A good way to explore Excel's many other functions is to select Reference Information from the Microsoft Excel Help Contents and then select Worksheet Functions. See Chapter 11.

High: =max(h4:h8)
Low:
Avg:

2 Enter the function =MAX(*range*) as shown here to display the largest number in the range.

High: 9
Low: =min(h4:h8)
Avg:

3 Enter the function =MIN(*range*) as shown here to display the smallest number in the range.

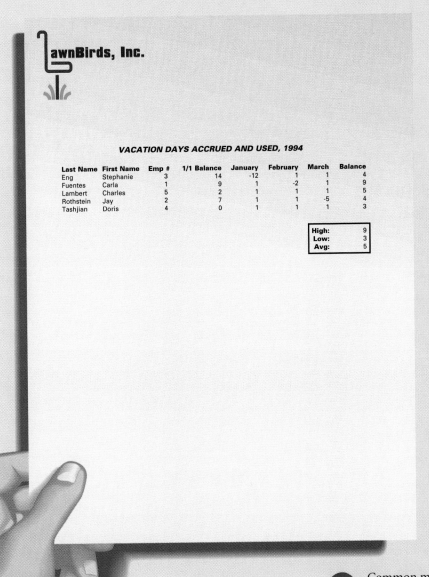

awnBirds, Inc.

VACATION DAYS ACCRUED AND USED, 1994

Last Name	First Name	Emp #	1/1 Balance	January	February	March	Balance
Eng	Stephanie	3	14	-12	1	1	4
Fuentes	Carla	1	9	1	-2	1	9
Lambert	Charles	5	2	1	1	1	5
Rothstein	Jay	2	7	1	1	-5	4
Tashjian	Doris	4	0	1	1	1	3

High:	9
Low:	3
Avg:	5

High: 9
Low: 3
Avg: =average(h4:h8)

4 Enter the function =AVERAGE(*range*) as shown here to display the average (arithmetic mean) of the numbers in the range. The AVERAGE function sums the numbers in the range and divides the result by the number of values summed.

Equal sign is missing.

Emp. #	1/1 Bal.	January
3	14	-12
1	9	1
5	2	1
2	7	1
4	0	1
High:	max(d4:d8)	

5 Common mistakes in entering functions include misspelling a function name and forgetting the equal sign and/or the opening parenthesis. (If you forget to type the closing parenthesis, Excel adds it for you.) Check for one of these mistakes if Excel tells you that you made an error or displays an obviously incorrect result, and edit the function as needed (see Chapter 5).

How to Fill In a Formula or Function

Many worksheets contain sequences of very similar formulas or functions. For example, the rightmost column in a table is often a sequence of SUM functions that present the totals of numbers to their left; the only difference from one function to the next is the row number. When building a worksheet, you could enter every formula and function in a separate procedure, but there's a much easier way to enter a sequence of formulas or functions when they are identical except for cell references. This technique is called *filling in* a row or column. When you fill in a row or column, Excel adjusts the cell references in the way it assumes you want it to—and it is usually correct.

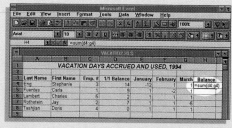

1 Enter the topmost or leftmost formula or function in the sequence.

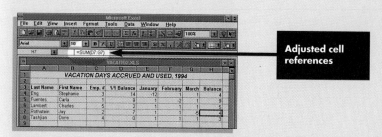

Adjusted cell references

6 Observe what has happened. In the cells, you see the formula or function results. Activate any filled-in cell and the formula bar will show you the formula or function that Excel inserted for you. Observe the cell references in the formula bar and notice how Excel adjusted them according to what it assumes you want.

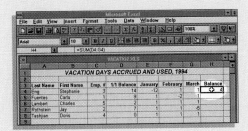

2 Activate the cell containing the formula or function.

3 Point to the little *x* in the bottom-right corner of the cell. Observe the shape of the mouse pointer.

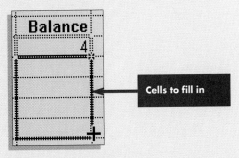

4 Drag the mouse down or to the right to select the cells you want to fill in with nearly identical formulas or functions.

5 Release the mouse button to fill in the cells.

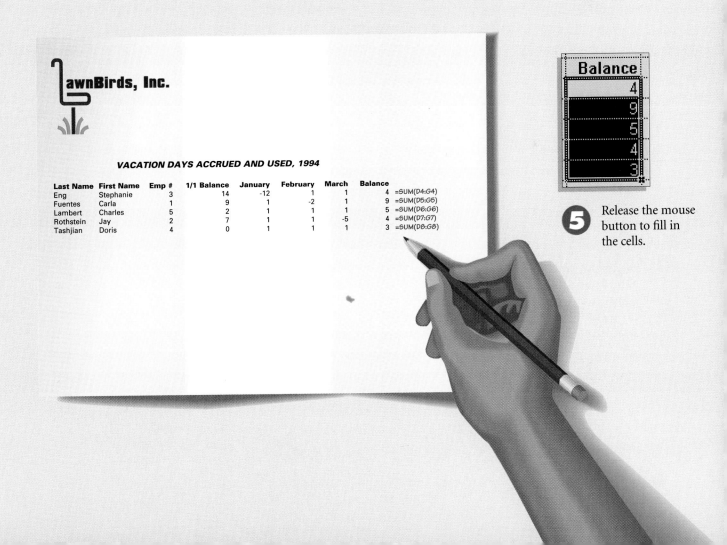

LawnBirds, Inc.

VACATION DAYS ACCRUED AND USED, 1994

Last Name	First Name	Emp #	1/1 Balance	January	February	March	Balance	
Eng	Stephanie	3	14	-12	1	1	4	=SUM(D4:G4)
Fuentes	Carla	1	9	1	-2	1	9	=SUM(D5:G5)
Lambert	Charles	5	2	1	1	1	5	=SUM(D6:G6)
Rothstein	Jay	2	7	1	1	-5	4	=SUM(D7:G7)
Tashjian	Doris	4	0	1	1	1	3	=SUM(D8:G8)

How to Work with Absolute References

Look at the sample worksheet on this page. Every number in the Bonus column represents a person's base pay multiplied by .07, or 7%, the multiplier entered at the bottom of the worksheet. You could enter Ms. Eng's bonus as =D6*B12, her base pay times the standard percentage. But what happens if you try to fill in the Bonus column as described on the preceding page, or if you copy the bonus formula to the other cells as described in Chapter 8? The reference to cell D6 increases automatically to D7, D8, and so on, just as you want. But the reference to the multiplier in cell B12 also increases to B13, B14, and so on, producing incorrect results. You need the reference to cell B12 to remain constant. To accomplish this, enter Ms. Eng's bonus calculation using an *absolute reference* to cell B12. Then, whenever the formula is used in a fill or copy operation, the reference will remain the same.

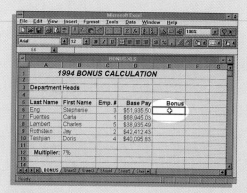

1 Activate the cell that contains (or will contain) the reference that you want to remain the same when copied.

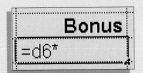

Bonus
=d6*

2 Begin typing or editing the formula or function normally.

Bonus
=d6*b12

3 To type the cell reference that is to remain constant in fill and copy operations, precede both the letter and the number with $ (the dollar sign).

awnBirds, Inc.

E6   =d6*b12

4 Enter the formula or function normally. The result appears in the cell.

	A	B	C	D	E
1	1994 BONUS CALCULATION				
2					
3	Department Heads				
4					
5	Last Name	First Name	Emp #	Base Pay	Bonus
6	Eng	Stephanie	3	$51,935.50	$3,635.49
7	Fuentes	Carla	1	$68,945.03	$4,826.15
8	Lambert	Charles	5	$38,935.49	$2,725.48
9	Rothstein	Jay	2	$42,412.43	$2,968.87
10	Tashjian	Doris	4	$40,095.83	$2,806.71
11					
12	Multiplier:	7%			

	A	B	C	D	E
1	1994 BONUS CALCULATION				
2					
3	Department Heads				
4					
5	Last Name	First Name	Emp. #	Base Pay	Bonus
6	Eng	Stephanie	3	$51,935.50	$3,635.49
7	Fuentes	Carla	1	$68,945.03	$4,826.15
8	Lambert	Charles	5	$38,935.49	$2,725.48
9	Rothstein	Jay	2	$42,412.43	$2,968.87
10	Tashjian	Doris	4	$40,095.83	$2,806.71
11					
12	Multiplier:	7%			

5 Use the formula or function as usual in fill operations (see preceding page) or copy operations (see Chapter 8).

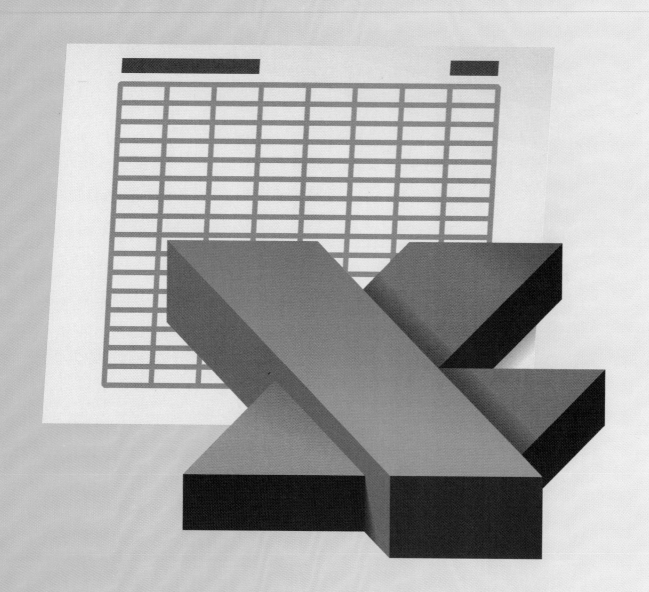

CHAPTER 11

Rescue

 Even the best-trained Excel user makes the occasional error or stumbles into unfamiliar territory. Far be it from Microsoft to abandon you in your time of need.

Excel's most valuable rescue feature is the Undo command, the first topic of this chapter. The Undo command reverses the last action you performed—entering cell contents, clearing cells, moving data, filling in a row or column, and so on. Though it cannot reverse every action, Undo is an excellent bet to get you out of hot water.

Excel also comes with volumes of *on-line help* that you can display on your screen and peruse much as you'd flip through a reference book. Excel's help system is *context-sensitive,* so it usually brings you directly to information on the action in progress. For example, if you issue the Help command when the Print dialog box is displayed, you see information about printing. This chapter explains how to issue the Help command and how to navigate the help system to find more information.

Finally, this chapter covers Excel's spelling checker, which can find and correct misspellings in cells that contain text.

How to Undo an Action

I f it hasn't happened to you yet, it will: You'll edit a formula incorrectly, move some cells when you meant to copy them, delete too many rows—and be dismayed or even horrified by the results. Not to worry. If you notice a mistake fast enough, you can probably reverse it instantly by issuing Excel's Undo command. The Undo command can reverse almost every worksheet building, editing, and formatting action. Beware, however, that Excel cannot undo certain actions, such as saving a workbook.

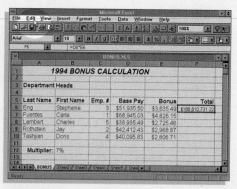

1 Click on Edit in the menu bar as soon as you realize that you want to undo your last action. Once you perform another action—even typing one character in a cell—the previous action becomes irreversible.

TIP SHEET

▶ Scrolling the worksheet, activating a different cell or sheet, and selecting a range do not make the previous action irreversible. For example, if you copy a formula and then activate a cell (but do nothing else), you can still undo the copy.

▶ All settings you make in one session with a dialog box constitute one action and thus can be reversed. Let's say you open the Font dialog box and assign a new font, style, and size to a cell (Chapter 9). The Undo command will reverse *all* these changes, not just the last one you selected.

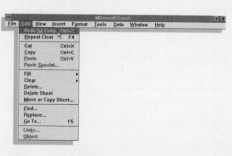

4 If the Undo command did not produce the result you expected, you can reverse it. Immediately click on Edit in the menu bar and then click on the Undo command, which now reads *Redo (u)* followed by the name of the action you just reversed. (The *u* tells you that after pulling down the Edit menu, you can type **u** instead of clicking on this command.)

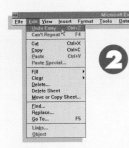

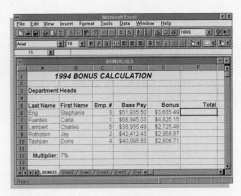

2 Observe the first command on the Edit menu. It reads *Undo* followed by the last action you took. If your last action is irreversible, the menu reads *Can't Undo*.

3 If the Undo command reflects the action you want to reverse, click on it. (Otherwise, click outside the menu to close it.)

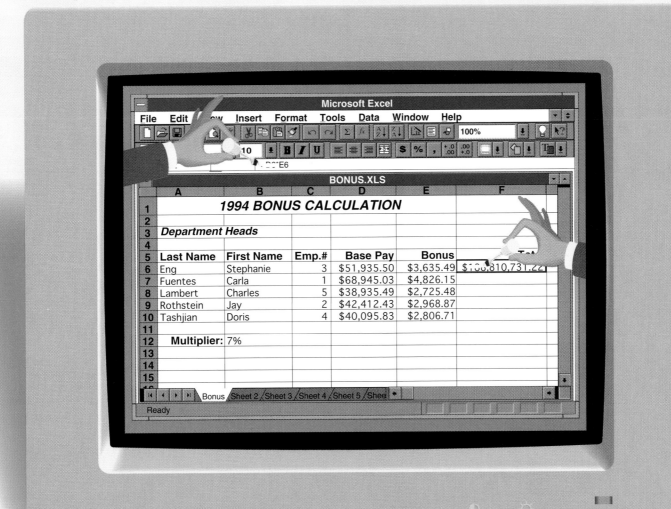

How to Get On-line Help

If you have questions as you work with Excel, you can turn to this book for help. But you may well be able to find the information you need without even taking your hands off the keyboard and mouse. Excel's Help command usually gives information related to the action in progress—and if it doesn't, you can search through the help system for the information you need. The Help command works at virtually all times, even when a menu is pulled down or a dialog box is displayed.

1 Press F1 to issue the Help command. If a dialog box was open, you see information about that dialog box. If a menu was pulled down, you see information about the highlighted command. If you were merely building or editing a worksheet, you see a general Microsoft Excel Help Contents screen.

TIP SHEET

▶ The Help window is an application window. You can maximize, minimize, restore, resize, and move it. One advantage of this fact is that you can arrange the Help window so that it does not cover the screen portion you need help with, such as a dialog box. See Chapter 2 for more information on window manipulation.

▶ An occasionally convenient way to get help with a command on Excel's menus is to press Shift+F1. The mouse pointer becomes an arrow with a question mark attached. Then, pull down the appropriate menu and click on the command with which you need help. Instead of issuing the command, you get a help screen on that command. Work with the help system as described on this page.

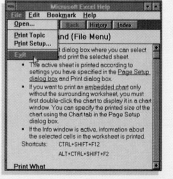

7 Observe that the help screen has its own menu bar, separate from Excel's. When done using the help system, click on File in the help system menu bar and then click on the Exit command.

2 Read the information, using the vertical scroll bar to scroll through it if necessary.

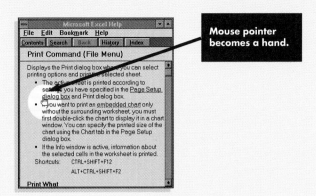

Mouse pointer becomes a hand.

3 To see more information about a solid-underlined topic, click on it. An entirely new help screen appears.

4 If you want to go back to the previous help screen, click on the Back button.

5 If you click on a solid-underlined topic and a How To window appears, read the information and then click on the Close button.

Definition

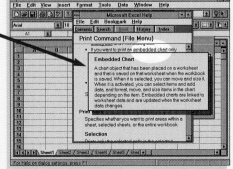

6 To see the definition of a dotted-underlined topic, click on it. A box containing the definition appears. Click anywhere to close the definition box.

How to Spell-Check a Worksheet

Excel comes with an electronic dictionary. Upon your command, Excel checks each word in the active worksheet against the dictionary. When it comes across a word that's not in the dictionary, Excel gives you a chance to correct it right away, and even gives you possible corrections to choose from. Since some correct spellings, such as proper names, unusual words, and foreign-language words, are not in the dictionary, you can tell Excel to skip over a word that it does not recognize.

TIP SHEET

▸ **Why not add every correctly spelled word to the dictionary? One reason is that adding words to the dictionary slows down the spelling checker. Don't slow it down with words you hardly ever use. The other reason is that a word can be a valid spelling in one context but not in another. For example, notice in step 3 that** *Gough* **is not added to the dictionary. That way, Excel will call attention to it in future spelling checks, where it might be a misspelling for** *Cough* **or** *Gouge.*

▸ **Excel's dictionary contains many common proper words including first names, last names, cities, states, countries, and geographical features.**

▸ **Beware that the spelling checker will not notice a misspelling that forms another legitimate word, such as misspelling** *than* **as** *then.* **Proofread your worksheets carefully to find this type of error.**

❶ *Only if* you want to check the spelling of less than the entire active sheet, select as a range the part you want to check.

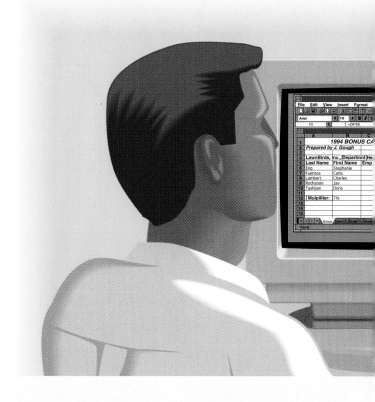

❽ Excel informs you when it is done with the spelling check. Click on the OK button.

❼ Unless you selected a range in step 1, Excel performs the spelling check from the active cell forward. If the active cell was not A1, Excel asks you whether you want to continue from the top of the worksheet. Click on Yes or No as desired.

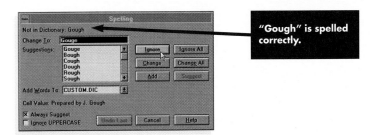

2 Click on Tools in the menu bar and then click on the Spelling command. The spelling check begins.

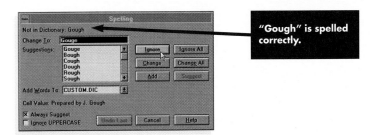

"Gough" is spelled correctly.

3 Excel presents the Spelling dialog box when it encounters a word that is not in the dictionary. If the word is spelled correctly but you don't use it often or it might be a misspelling in another context, click on either the Ignore button or the Ignore All button. The Ignore button simply continues the spelling check, skipping over the word in this instance. The Ignore All button skips over the word wherever it appears for the rest of this spelling check.

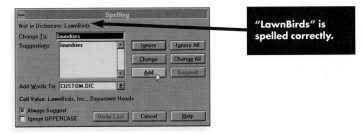

"LawnBirds" is spelled correctly.

4 If the word is spelled correctly and you plan to use it frequently in other worksheets, click on the Add button. This adds the word to Excel's electronic dictionary and continues the spelling check.

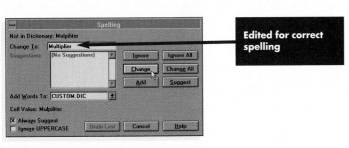

Edited for correct spelling

6 If the word is misspelled but the correct spelling does not appear in the Suggestions list, click on the Change To text box and use normal editing techniques (Backspace, Delete, the typing keys) to correct the word. Then click on the Change button to continue the spelling check.

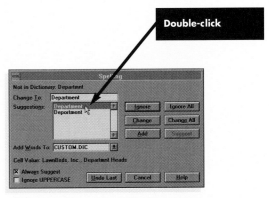

Double-click

5 If the word is misspelled and you see the correct spelling in the Suggestions list, double-click on that spelling to correct the word and continue the spelling check.

TRY IT!

You've built up quite a set of Excel skills in the last four chapters of this book. Now here is an opportunity to get some hands-on practice. Follow these steps at your computer to produce the worksheet shown below. Most steps include chapter numbers to help you find more information on the skills required. When formatting the sheet, remember that the available fonts, styles, and point sizes can differ from one computer to the next, so your sheet may not match the one shown here in every detail.

1

Start Excel if it is not already running. Unless you already have a blank worksheet on your screen, start a new sheet by clicking on File in the menu bar and then clicking on the New command. *Chapter 6*

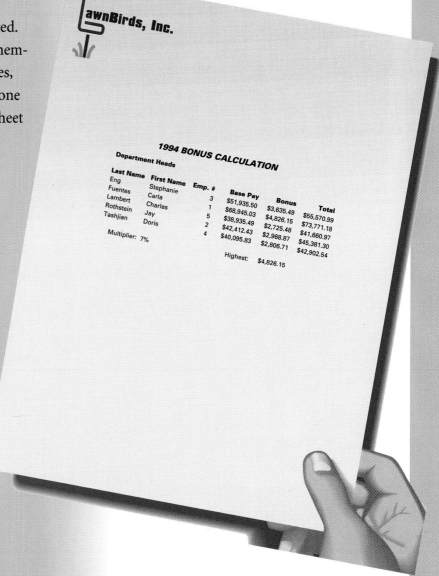

LawnBirds, Inc.

1994 BONUS CALCULATION

Department Heads

Last Name	First Name	Emp. #	Base Pay	Bonus	Total
Eng	Stephanie	3	$51,935.50	$3,635.49	$55,570.99
Fuentes	Carla	1	$68,945.03	$4,826.15	$73,771.18
Lambert	Charles	5	$38,935.49	$2,725.48	$41,660.97
Rothstein	Jay	2	$42,412.43	$2,968.87	$45,381.30
Tashjian	Doris	4	$40,095.83	$2,806.71	$42,902.54

Multiplier: 7%

Highest: $4,826.15

Enter the basic sheet exactly as shown here. All numbers are plain data, not formula or function results.

	A	B	C	D	E
1	1994 BONUS CALCULATION				
2					
3	Department Heads				
4					
5	Name	Emp. #	Base Pay	Bonus	Total
6	Eng	3	51935.5		
7	Fuentes	1	68945.03		
8	Lambert	5	38935.49		
9	Rothstein	2	42412.43		
10	Tashjian	4	40095.83		
11					
12	Multiplier:		7%		

Click on File in the menu bar and then click on the Save command.

```
File
New            Ctrl+N
Open...         Ctrl+O
Close
Save            Ctrl+S
Save As...
Save Workspace...
Find File...
Summary Info...
Page Setup...
Print Preview
Print...         Ctrl+P
Print Report...
1 TEST.XLS
2 SECONDQ.XLS
3 ABC.XLS
4 JUNE.XLS
Exit
```

In the File Name area of the Save As dialog box, type **bonus** to save the workbook as BONUS.XLS. Then click on the OK button. *Chapter 6*

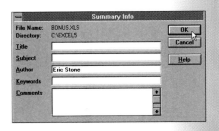

5

If the Summary Info dialog box appears, click on the OK button.

6

Select the Base Pay numbers and the blank cells beneath the Bonus and Total headings. *Chapter 5*

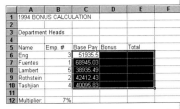

	A	B	C	D	E	F
1	1994 BONUS CALCULATION					
2						
3	Department Heads					
4						
5	Name	Emp. #	Base Pay	Bonus	Total	
6	Eng	3	51935.5			
7	Fuentes	1	68945.03			
8	Lambert	5	38935.49			
9	Rothstein	2	42412.43			
10	Tashjian	4	40095.83			
11						
12	Multiplier:		7%			

Click on Format in the menu bar and then click on the Cells command to display the Format Cells dialog box. *Chapter 9*

```
Format
Cells...   Ctrl+1
Row          ▶
Column       ▶
Sheet        ▶
AutoFormat...
Style...
Placement    ▶
```

Click on the Number tab if necessary. In the Category list, click on Currency. In the Format Codes list, click on the last currency formatting option. Then click on the OK button to apply this format to the numbers now in the Base Pay column and to the numbers that will later appear in the Bonus and Total columns. *Chapter 9*

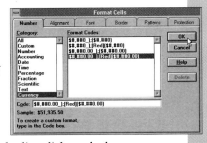

Column C is now too narrow to display its contents, so it displays pound signs (#####) instead. Point to the right border of column heading C and drag to the right, widening the column enough to display its contents. Use the same technique to widen columns D and E about the same amount, since they will contain numbers about as wide as those in column C. *Chapter 8*

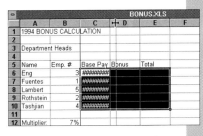

Continue to next page ▶

TRY IT!

Continue
below

Select the
range A3:E5.
Then click on
Format in the
menu bar

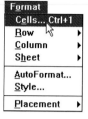

and click on the Cells command to
display the Format Cells dialog box.
Chapter 9

Click on the
Font tab. In
the Font
Style list,
click on Bold.
Then click on

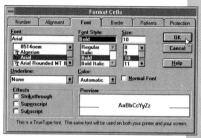

the OK button to boldface the selected
cells. *Chapter 9*

Bonus
=c6*b12

Activate cell D6, type **=c6*b12** and
click on the enter box. The dollar
signs in this formula produce an absolute reference, so that when you
copy this formula to other cells, the
reference to the multiplier in cell B12
will not change. *Chapter 10*

Base Pay	Bonus	Total
$51,935.50	$3,635.49	
$68,945.03	$4,826.15	
$38,935.49	$2,725.48	
$42,412.43	$2,968.87	
$40,095.83	$2,806.71	

With cell D6
active, point to
the bottom-
right corner of the cell so that the
mouse pointer becomes a thin, solid
cross. Then drag down to fill in the four
cells below D6. Release the mouse button and observe that each filled-in cell
multiplies the cell to its left by the multiplier in cell B12. *Chapter 10*

Activate any
cell in col-
umn B. Then
click on
Insert in the
menu bar
and click on
the Columns
command.
Chapter 8

Activate cell
E6 and enter
the formula
=c6+d6 to
calculate
Eng's total pay. Then, with cell E6 still
active, point to the bottom-right corner
of the cell and drag down to fill in the
four cells below it. *Chapter 10*

As shown,
enter the con-
tents of the
newly created
column B.
Also, edit cell
A5 to read
Last Name
(Chapter 5). Finally, widen columns A
and B as needed by dragging the right
border of each column heading. *Chapter 8*

	A	B	C
1	1994 BONUS CALCULATION		
2			
3	Department Heads		
4			
5	Last Name	First Name	Emp. #
6	Eng	Stephanie	3
7	Fuentes	Carla	1
8	Lambert	Charles	5
9	Rothstein	Jay	2
10	Tashjian	Doris	4
11			
12	Multiplier:		7%

17

Activate cell C12, point to the cell border so that the mouse pointer becomes an arrow, drag one cell to the left, and release the mouse button to move the cell contents. *Chapter 8*

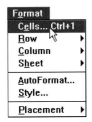
18

Select the range C5:F5, click on Format in the menu bar, and then click on the Cells command. *Chapter 9*

19

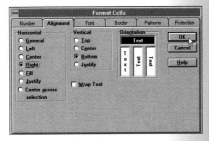

Click on the Alignment tab, click on the Right radio button, and then click on the OK button to right-align the contents of these cells with their cell borders. *Chapter 9*

20

Using the same technique as in the two preceding steps, right-align cell A12, and left-align cell B12. Hint: To change the alignment of one cell, simply activate the cell; do not select a range. *Chapter 9*

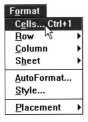
21

Activate cell A1, click on Format in the menu bar, and then click on the Cells command. *Chapter 9*

22

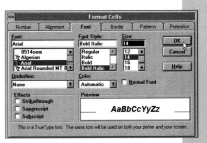

Click on the Font tab, click on Bold Italic in the Font Style list, click on 14 in the Size list, and then click on the OK button. *Chapter 9*

23

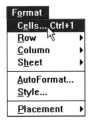

Select the range A1:F1, click on Format in the menu bar, and then click on the Cells command. *Chapter 9*

24

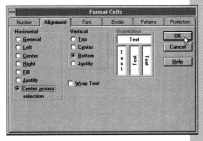

Click on the Alignment tab, click on the Center across Selection radio button, and then click on the OK button. *Chapter 9*

25

Base Pay	Bonus	Total
$51,935.50	$3,635.49	$55,570.99
$68,945.03	$4,826.15	$73,771.18
$38,935.49	$2,725.48	$41,660.97
$42,412.43	$2,968.87	$45,381.30
$40,095.83	$2,806.71	$42,902.54
Highest:	=max(e6:e10)	

In cell D12, enter **Highest:** and right-align the cell contents. (Click on Format, click on Cells, click on the Alignment tab, click on the Right radio button, and click on the OK button.) In cell E12, enter the function =**max(e6:e10)** to display the highest bonus given. *Chapter 10*

26

Resave the worksheet, print it if you so desire, and close it. *Chapter 6*

CHAPTER 12

Charts

 You probably have a pretty good understanding of the business data you work with. (You should, anyway!) But hand a printout of an Excel worksheet to a colleague or show a worksheet to a client in a presentation and you may get a puzzled reaction. Columns and rows of numbers are not always the best way to give someone information at a glance.

That's where charts (often called graphs) come in. A good chart makes data visually meaningful. By emphasizing trends and comparative factors, a chart tells a story quickly and concisely.

Excel can instantly express all or part of your data in one of several popular chart types. Even better, as you edit the data on which the chart is based, the chart is updated instantly to reflect the new data. This chapter explains how to create, improve, and manage charts based on your Excel worksheet data.

How to Create a Chart

Excel guides you step by step through the charting process, asking you what data to chart, what type of chart to create, and what special features, such as a legend or a chart title, to add. This page explains how to create a chart. The rest of this chapter helps you change the chart type and improve chart appearance.

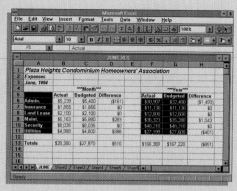

1 Select the data, column headings, and row headings you want to chart. Often, as in the example here, you need to select a noncontiguous range (see Chapter 5). Also, carefully consider whether you want to include rows and columns containing totals in the chart; frequently, as in the example on this page, you don't.

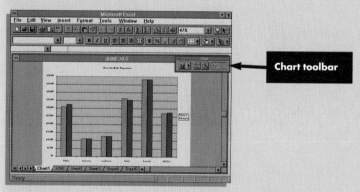

Chart toolbar

8 Excel places your chart in a chart sheet that is added to your workbook. To go back to the sheet containing your data, simply click on its worksheet tab.

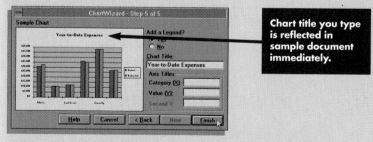

Chart title you type is reflected in sample document immediately.

7 Specify whether you want the chart to have a legend. If you want a chart title, type it in the Chart Title text box. If you chose a chart type that has axes and you want a title running along the x-axis and/or y-axis, type each title in the appropriate Axis Titles text box. When done, click on the Finish button.

TIP SHEET

► **Starting at the second dialog box in the chart creation process, you can click on the Back button to backtrack and make different selections. To change a chart you've finished creating, see the upcoming pages of this chapter. To abandon the chart creation process at any stage, click on the Cancel button or press the Escape key.**

► **Excel names your first chart sheet in the workbook Chart1, the second, Chart2, and so on. You can rename a chart sheet the same way you rename a worksheet. The easiest way is to double-click on the sheet tab, type a new name in the Rename Sheet dialog box, and click on the OK button.**

► **You can print a chart the same way you print any sheet in the workbook. See Chapter 7.**

2 Click on Insert in the menu bar, click on the Chart command, and then click on As New Sheet. You will place the chart on a new sheet called a *chart sheet*.

3 Excel asks you to confirm that the selected cells are the ones you want charted. Click on the Next button.

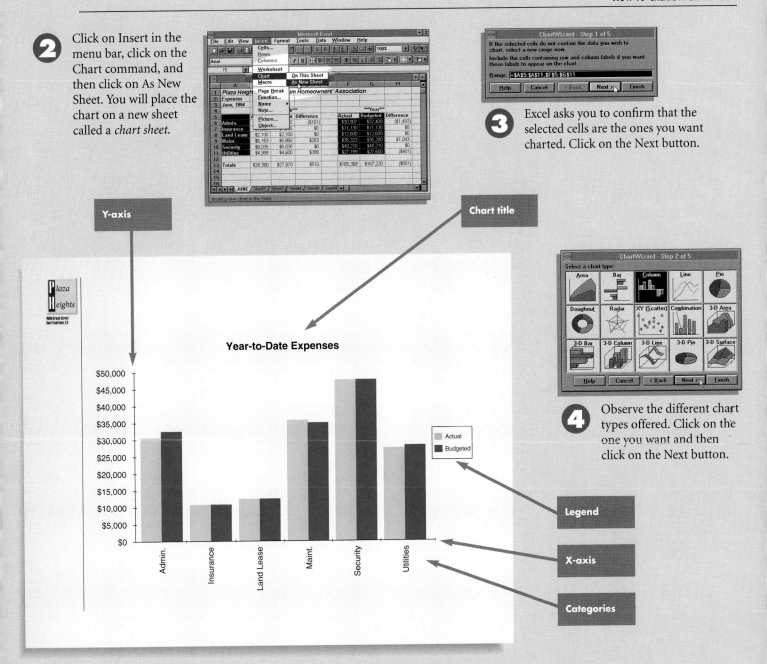

Y-axis

Chart title

Legend

X-axis

Categories

Year-to-Date Expenses

4 Observe the different chart types offered. Click on the one you want and then click on the Next button.

5 Within each chart type, Excel offers several variations. Click on the one you want and then click on the Next button.

6 Look at the sample chart in this dialog box and see if Excel has interpreted the organization of your data correctly. You may have to tell Excel to take the data series from rows in your worksheet rather than columns, or to use the content of one or more different columns or rows to supply the chart labels, the legend text, or the chart title. (The questions in this dialog box vary slightly by chart type.) When done, click on the Next button.

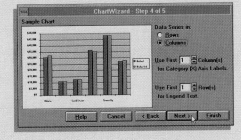

How to Change the Chart Type

The dizzying array of chart types offered by Excel means that people sometimes have trouble settling on just the right type of chart to express their data. If you haven't studied graphs since sometime back in your school days, you may not even recognize the names of some of the chart types. Fortunately, Excel lends itself to trial and error, making it easy to change the chart type.

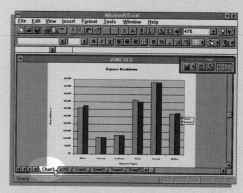

1 Activate the sheet containing the chart you want to change.

▶ Excel's three-dimensional charts are impressive works of art, but they are not suitable for every purpose. In particular, black-and-white print-outs of three-dimensional charts are sometimes awkward-looking or difficult to interpret.

▶ As you experiment with different chart types, you may wish to adjust the magnification level of the chart sheet so you can get a better idea of what Excel has done to the chart. In particular, it is often helpful to zoom in closer (make the chart look bigger) so that you can read the labels and titles on the chart. Click on View in the menu bar and then click on the Zoom command. In the Zoom dialog box, click on the desired magnification level, such as 100%, and then click on the OK button.

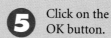

5 Click on the OK button.

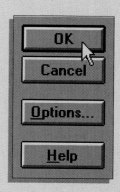

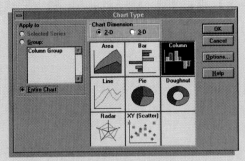

2 Click on Format in the menu bar and then click on the Chart Type command. (Observe that Excel's menus contain some different commands when the active sheet is a chart sheet.)

3 Excel offers both plain two-dimensional charts and charts with fancy effects that simulate a third dimension. If you want to switch from a two-dimensional chart type to a three-dimensional type, click on the 3-D radio button. Likewise, click on the 2-D radio button to go from three-dimensional chart types to two-dimensional ones.

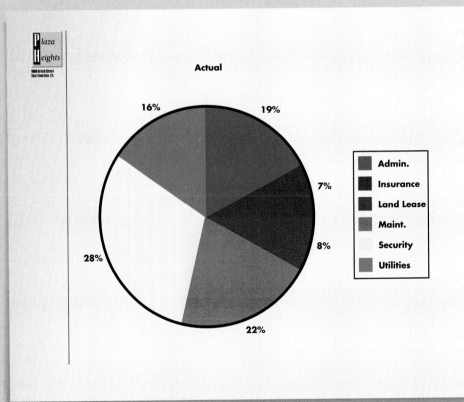

4 Click on the chart type you want.

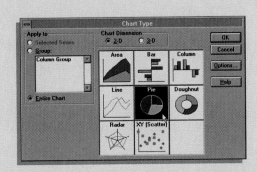

How to Work with Chart and Axis Titles

Y ou can specify a chart title, an x-axis title, and a y-axis title while creating your chart, as explained earlier in this chapter. But it is also easy to add, change, and delete these titles later. This page explains how.

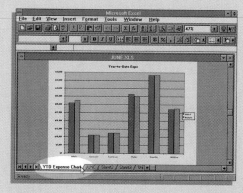

1 Activate the sheet containing the chart whose titles you want to work with.

8 To delete a chart or axis title, click on it to display its selection squares and then press the Delete key.

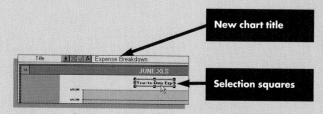

New chart title

Selection squares

7 To change a chart or axis title, click on it. The *selection squares* surrounding the title indicate that it is now subject to editing. Type the new title and press Enter.

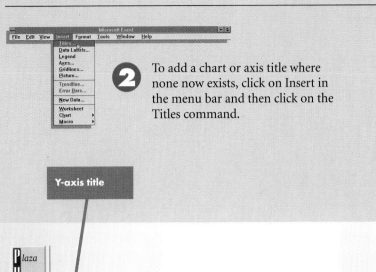

2 To add a chart or axis title where none now exists, click on Insert in the menu bar and then click on the Titles command.

3 In the Titles dialog box, mark the check box for the title you want to add: Chart Title, Value (Y) Axis, or Category (X) Axis.

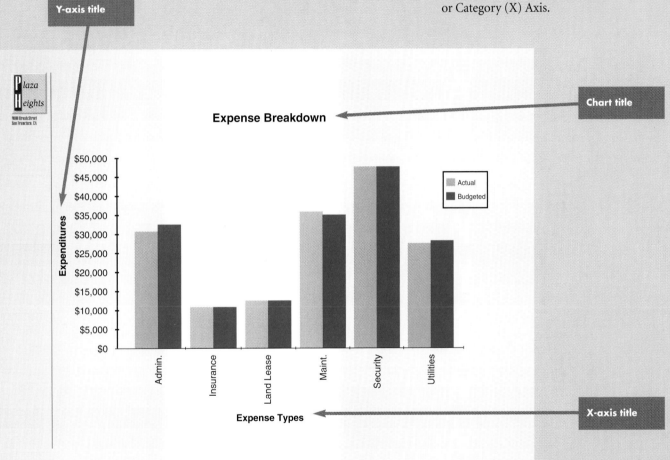

Y-axis title

Chart title

X-axis title

5 Type the title and press Enter.

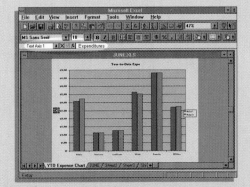

4 Click on the OK button.

6 Repeat steps 2 through 5 to add additional titles as needed.

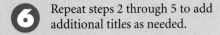

CHAPTER 13

Searching for Data

 Excel worksheets can also be called *electronic databases*. They contain data organized, with the help of a computer, into logically related rows and columns. You have probably been working with databases—though perhaps not electronic ones—for years: address books, client records, inventories, and so on. People and businesses have put many databases on computers because computers make data easier to find, sort, change, delete, and so on.

This chapter and the next focus on Excel's database management capabilities. In this chapter, you will learn how to search for data that meet a certain condition. For example, in a large worksheet containing pay records for all your company personnel, you can have Excel instantly find the data for an employee named Lambert, or for all employees earning under $40,000 per year, or for everyone in the marketing department.

Before proceeding, make sure you're comfortable with certain fundamental database terms. A *record* is all the data about one subject—all the personnel data about Lambert, all the sales information about one product, and so on. A *field* is a data category. For example, fields in a personnel database might include name, Social Security number, date of hire, and pay rate. In standard databases such as those used as examples in this book, each record is one row and each field is one column. The column headings are often called *field names*.

How to Set Up a Search

Excel's *AutoFilter* command can quickly display only those database records that meet a certain condition, temporarily "filtering out" all other records. Once you filter your database, you can view, edit, copy, or print the remaining records, just as you do with any data in Excel. Because the AutoFilter command adds some strange elements to the Excel interface, this page simply gets you familiar with AutoFilter. The next page shows you how to filter your data.

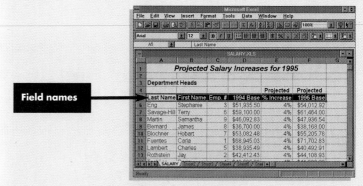

Field names

1 Select the field names (column headings) in your database. If any column headings occupy more than one row, select only the bottom row.

▶ Until you get accustomed to the AutoFilter drop-down arrows, it can be disconcerting to have them on the screen. If you display the arrows but decide not to filter the database just yet, click on Data, click on Filter, and click on AutoFilter to hide the arrows.

▶ You can edit cell contents as usual when the cell has an AutoFilter drop-down arrow.

6 Now that you know how to set up an AutoFilter, see the next page to learn how to filter your database.

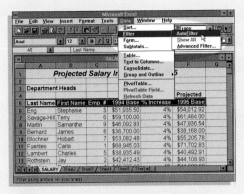

2 Click on Data in the menu bar, click on Filter, and then click on the AutoFilter command.

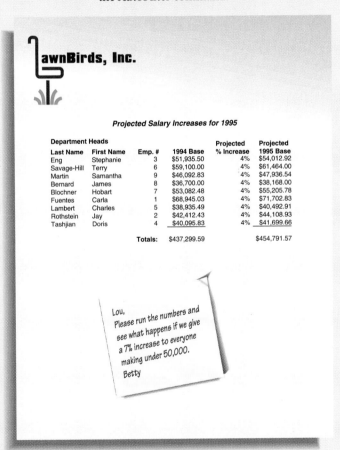

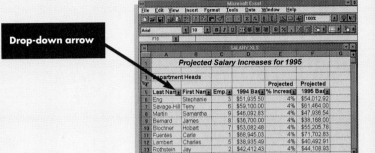

Drop-down arrow

3 Each field name now has a *drop-down arrow* in it.

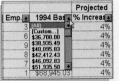

4 Click on any drop-down arrow. The list that appears shows the content of each cell in the column, plus some special entries like *(All)* and *(Custom)*. The next page explains what this list means.

5 As with any drop-down list in Windows, click outside the list or press Escape to close it without making a selection.

How to Perform a Search

To perform a search, you give Excel a criterion against which to test every record in the database. The criterion could be records where the department name is Marketing, records where the salary is less than $50,000—whatever meets your data needs. Only records that meet the criterion remain displayed. This page explains how to state the criterion and perform the search.

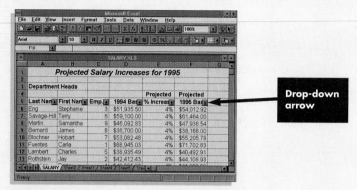

Drop-down arrow

1 Display the AutoFilter drop-down arrows as described on the preceding page.

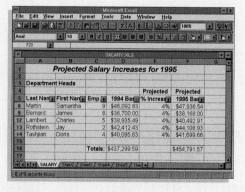

8 View, edit, copy, and print the filtered database the same way you work with any Excel data. Excel changes the color of the row numbers in a filtered list to remind you that you are not viewing the complete database.

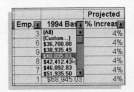

2 Click on the arrow for the field you are testing. For example, if you want to filter out records based on a certain salary level, click on the arrow for the salary field.

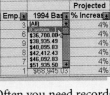

3 If you want to view all records where a certain value exists for this field, click on that value in the list. For example, you might drop down a list for a field named Department and click on Marketing to display personnel records of people who work in your marketing department, filtering out everyone else. Excel immediately filters the list, displaying only the records that meet the condition. Skip to step 8.

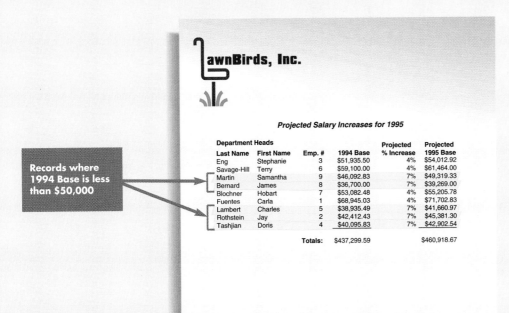

Records where 1994 Base is less than $50,000

4 Often you need records meeting a more complex criterion, such as all employees with a salary under a certain amount. After clicking on the drop-down arrow of the appropriate field, click on *(Custom)*.

5 In the Custom AutoFilter dialog box, type the number or text against which to test each record.

7 Click on the OK button to filter the database.

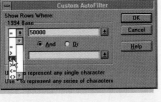

6 Specify the way records should be tested against this number or text. All standard comparison operators are available: equal to (=), greater than (>), less than (<), greater than or equal to (>=), less than or equal to (<=), and not equal to (<>).

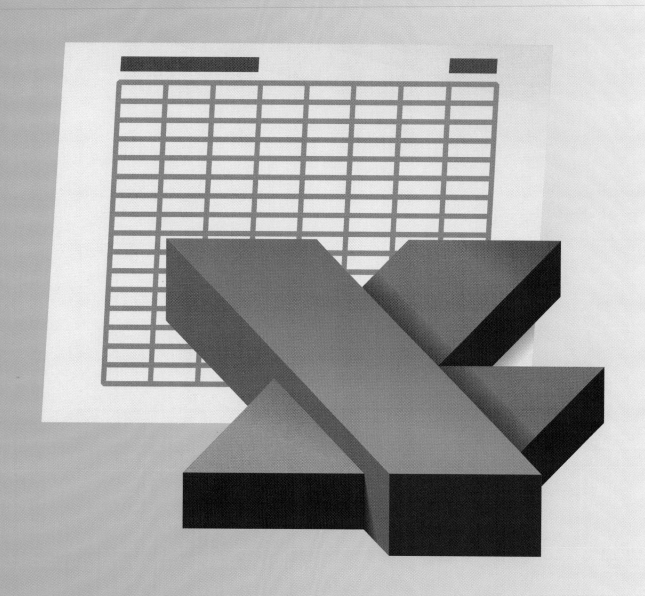

CHAPTER 14

Sorting Data

 Most worksheets are easier to work with and more presentable when there is some sense to the sequence of rows. For example, personnel worksheets usually are arranged alphabetically by employee's last name, or perhaps in numerical order by employee identification number.

You might try building a worksheet in the sequence you need, but as you add, delete, and edit data, it is bound to fall out of order. Moving rows around to restore order could be nightmarish indeed. Instead, use Excel's highly capable Sort command. It can instantly sort your data according to the content of any column you choose.

Some terminology: A sort *key* is the column whose content is the basis for the sort. For example, if a personnel worksheet contains columns for last name, Social Security number, salary, and hire date, and you sort the worksheet according to salary, the salary column is the sort key. Excel allows you up to three keys per sort. When the first key results in a tie—two or more employees with the same salary—the optional second key kicks in, perhaps sorting by last name those employees with identical salaries. The optional third key could sort by Social Security number any employees who have both the same salary and the same last name.

By default, Excel sorts in ascending order: lowest number to highest for a key containing numbers, and standard alphabetical order for a key containing text. However, you can specify that a key work in descending order—for example, arranging employees from highest salary to lowest.

How to Sort Data

Sorting data involves telling Excel what to sort, what keys to use, and whether to sort in ascending or descending order. As you'll observe, the Sort command, while easy to issue, subjects you to certain pitfalls and makes quite significant changes to your worksheet. Though you should always be careful when working with important business data, be extra careful when setting up a sort operation. You can reverse a sort with the Undo command (Chapter 11), but only if you catch your mistake before performing another action.

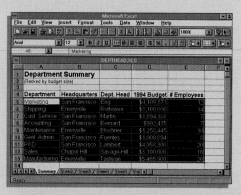

1 Select the data you want to sort. Be sure to select entire data records; only selected cells are moved in a sort, so if you select partial rows, some cells in a record will shift while others stay put. Selecting column headings is optional. However, if some of your column headings occupy more than one row, do not select column headings at all.

TIP SHEET

▶ **It's smart to save your worksheet immediately before performing a sort. That way, if the sort goes awry and you notice the problem too late to perform an undo, you can close the worksheet *without* saving it and then reopen it (see Chapter 6). The reopened worksheet will be exactly as you last saved it—before the defective sort.**

▶ **Sorting the result of an AutoFilter—and then perhaps printing or charting it—is a great way to pull out little snippets of data for presentation. For example, from a personnel worksheet, you could filter a list of employees with more than 5 years of service (see Chapter 13) and then sort the resulting list in descending order by years of service.**

▶ **Instead of selecting the database in step 1, you could simply activate any cell in the database. Then, when you issue the Sort command in step 2, Excel will figure out the boundaries of your database. However, Excel does not always make this determination correctly, so it is safest to select the database and remove any doubt.**

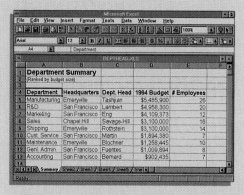

8 Immediately inspect the results of the sort. If you did not get the results you expected—maybe in step 1 you mistakenly selected incomplete records—select Edit and then select the Undo command. The Undo command completely reverses a sort operation so you can start over from scratch.

7 Click on the OK button to perform the sort.

2 Click on Data and then click on Sort.

3 In the Sort dialog box, make sure Excel has correctly determined whether your database has a header row (column headings). If necessary, click on the Header Row or No Header Row radio button.

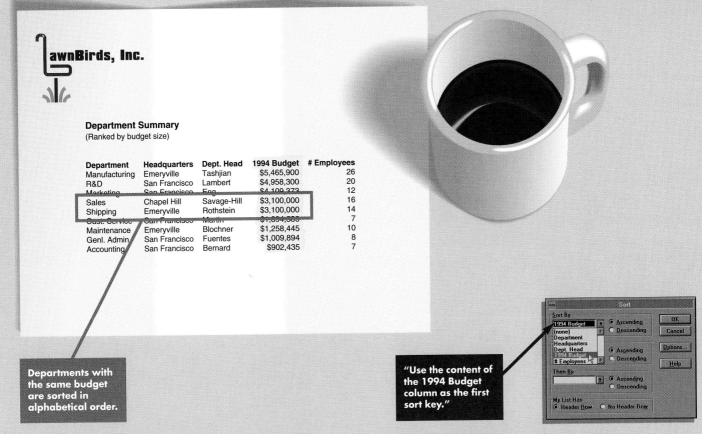

LawnBirds, Inc.

Department Summary
(Ranked by budget size)

Department	Headquarters	Dept. Head	1994 Budget	# Employees
Manufacturing	Emeryville	Tashjian	$5,465,900	26
R&D	San Francisco	Lambert	$4,958,300	20
Marketing	San Francisco	Eng	$4,100,373	12
Sales	Chapel Hill	Savage-Hill	$3,100,000	16
Shipping	Emeryville	Rothstein	$3,100,000	14
Cust. Service	San Francisco	Martin	$1,334,000	7
Maintenance	Emeryville	Blochner	$1,258,445	10
Genl. Admin.	San Francisco	Fuentes	$1,009,894	8
Accounting	San Francisco	Bernard	$902,435	7

Departments with the same budget are sorted in alphabetical order.

"Use the content of the 1994 Budget column as the first sort key."

4 In the Sort By area, observe the field name (column heading) Excel has inserted as the default first key. If you want to use this column as the first sort key, skip this step. Otherwise, click on the drop-down arrow and select the column to use as the first sort key.

"If the first key results in any ties, sort the ties using the Department column as the key."

"Sort from highest to lowest."

6 If you want to have one or two more sort keys to break ties produced by the first key, repeat steps 4 and 5 to specify a sort key and sort order (ascending or descending) in the first and, if necessary, the second Then By area.

5 By default, Excel sorts in ascending order. If you want this key to sort in descending order, mark the Descending radio button in the Sort By area.

TRY IT!

Here is a chance to sharpen your Excel skills—especially the database management operations covered in the preceding two chapters. Follow the steps given to build a database, search for data that meet certain criteria, and sort the data. Chapter numbers are included to help you find more information on the skills required for most steps.

Start a new workbook and save it as SUPPORT.XLS. *Chapter 6*

 LawnBirds, Inc.

Total Product Support Allocation

Product Name	Product Code #	% of 1Q 1994 Sales	1994 Support Budget	1995 Support (Est.)
Classic Pink	2355	21%	$104,300	$119,515
Coral Gables	4352	8%	$68,300	$71,715
Econo-Bird	3530	16%	$62,600	$65,730
Old Reliable	5034	28%	$108,900	$134,345
The Acrobat	1595	4%	$29,900	$31,395
Wingspan	8242	10%	$60,100	$63,105
Yard Monarch	9053	13%	$51,500	$54,075

Products with 10% or less of sales, and their projected 1995 product support allocation

Product Name	% of 1Q 1994 Sales	1995 Support (Est.)
Wingspan	10%	$63,105
Coral Gables	8%	$71,715
The Acrobat	4%	$31,395

2

Enter the basic, unformatted worksheet shown here. All

numbers are plain data, not formula or function results. Widen columns by dragging the right column border as needed so you can see the complete cell contents. *Chapter 8*

3

Double-click on the active worksheet tab. *Chapter 6*

4

In the Rename Sheet dialog box, type **Support** and click on the OK button. *Chapter 6*

5

Format the main headline as Arial bold italic 18-point, the column headings as Arial bold 12-point, and the rest of the database as Arial 12-point. Reminder: Select the Cells command from the Format menu and click on the Font tab at the top of the Format Cells dialog box. When done, drag the right column borders to widen columns as needed. *Chapter 9*

6

Right-align the range B3:E4. Reminder: Select the Cells command from the Format menu and click on the Alignment tab. *Chapter 9*

7

Select the range A4:E4, the bottom row of the column headings.

8

Click on Data, click on Filter, and then click on AutoFilter to add a drop-down arrow to each selected cell. *Chapter 13*

9

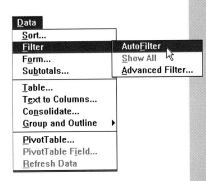

Click on the drop-down arrow in the 1994 Sales cell, and then click on (Custom...). *Chapter 13*

Continue to next page ▶

TRY IT!

Continue below

In the top text box of the Custom AutoFilter dialog box, type **20%**. *Chapter 13*

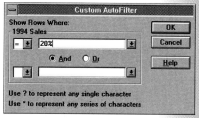

11

Click on the drop-down arrow to the left of this text box and click on >=. *Chapter 13*

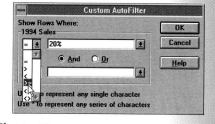

12

Click on the OK button.

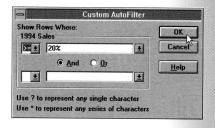

13

Observe that Excel has filtered out all but the two records that had a number greater than or equal to 20%. Let's say you want to add another $10,000 to the estimated 1995 support budget for these best-selling products. Edit cell E5 to read **$119,515** and cell E8 to read **$134,345**. *Chapter 5*

14

In cells A14 and A15, enter the two-row heading shown and format it to Arial bold 14-point. Reminder: Select both cells, click on Format, click on Cells, and click on the Font tab. *Chapter 9*

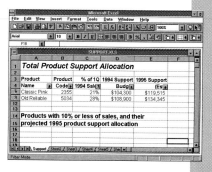

15

Repeat steps 9 through 12, but this time find all records where % of 1Q 1994 Sales is less than or equal to 10%. Three records meet this criterion. *Chapter 13*

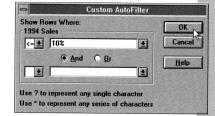

16

Select the column headings and the three records produced by the AutoFilter. Then point to the border of the selected range so that the mouse pointer becomes an arrow. *Chapter 8*

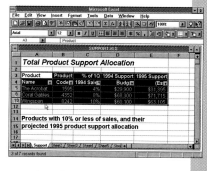

17

Drag down so that the top-left corner of the outlined area is over cell A17, hold down the Control key, and then release the mouse button to copy the headings and records. *Chapter 8*

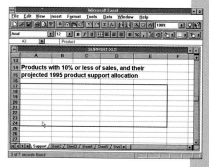

Click on Data, click on Filter, and then click on the AutoFilter command to get rid of the drop-down arrows and show all records in the main database. *Chapter 13.*

In the small database you just created at the bottom of the sheet, delete the Product Code # and 1994 Support Budget columns. Use the Delete command on the Edit menu, not the Delete key (Chapter 8). When done, drag the right column borders to widen columns as needed. *Chapter 9*

17	Product	% of 1Q	1995 Support
18	Name	1994 Sales	(Est.)
19	The Acrobat	4%	$31,395
20	Coral Gables	8%	$71,715
21	Wingspan	10%	$63,105

Select the three records in the small database.

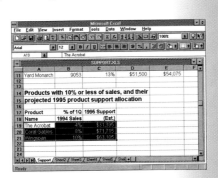

Click on Data and then click on Sort.
Chapter 14

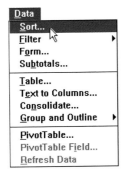

In the Sort dialog box, specify that you want to sort by the 1994 Sales column in descending order, and then click on the OK button.
Chapter 14

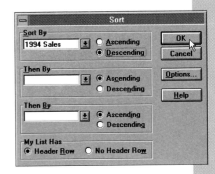

Select the main database near the top of the work-sheet, click on Data, and click on Sort.
Chapter 14

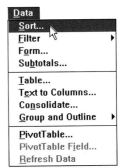

Sort this data-base in as-cending order by the Name column.
Chapter 14

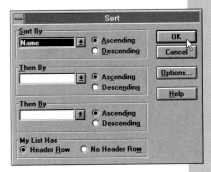

Save, print, and close the workbook.

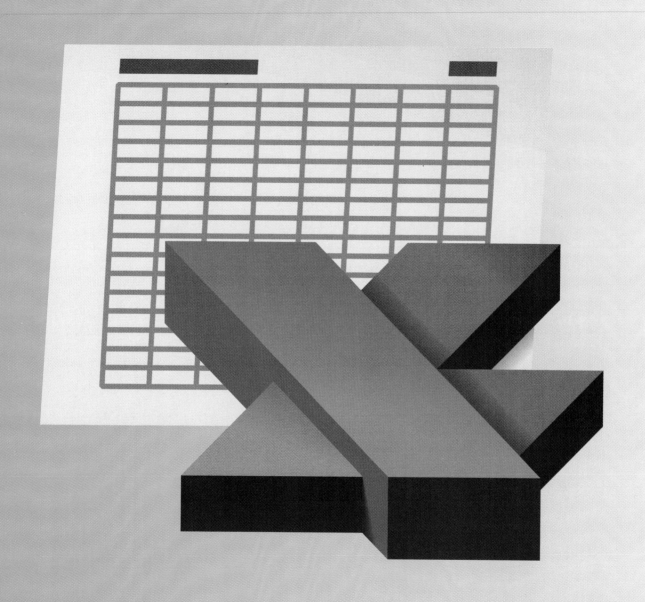

CHAPTER 15

Shortcuts

 Did you ever ask for driving directions in an unfamiliar city? The less familiar you were with the territory, the more likely you wanted to know the easiest, least confusing way to go—even if it wasn't the fastest. Only when you are comfortable with the general layout of a city are you interested in shortcuts.

Learning to use software is a similar experience. That's why this book really is not about shortcuts. Since you started out as an inexperienced user, this book has assumed you want to know one way—the most straightforward way—to get the job done.

But now that you are comfortable with Excel, you are ready to sample the many convenient shortcuts available from its *Standard toolbar* and *Formatting toolbar*. Some of these shortcuts can save you considerable effort over the long run and are certainly worth the time it takes to learn about them. Others—shortcuts that address tasks you perform infrequently—you may want to skip. Use of the toolbars is entirely optional.

How to Issue Commands from the Standard Toolbar

The Standard toolbar sits right below the menu bar. It contains tools that substitute for commands you otherwise issue from the menu bar and from dialog boxes. To use a tool, simply click on it. This page describes only those tools that provide shortcuts to tasks covered in this book.

TIP SHEET

▶ **Display of the Standard toolbar is optional. If it does not appear on your screen, click on Views, click on Toolbars, mark the Standard check box in the Toolbars dialog box, and then click on the OK button. To hide the toolbar if you don't use it, follow the same steps but this time clear the Standard check box. By hiding the toolbar, you gain space to show a little more of your worksheet in the window.**

▶ **If your Standard toolbar looks different from the one shown on this page, then someone—perhaps a consultant or an office computer whiz—has customized it. You can reset the Standard toolbar to look the way it originally did, but first you should find out why it was customized and make sure you're not violating workgroup policy or eliminating tools you'd find useful if you knew what they were. To reset the Standard toolbar, click on View, click on Toolbars, click on Standard in the Toolbars dialog box, click on the Reset button, make sure the Standard check box remains marked, and then click on the OK button.**

▶ **If you have a customized Standard toolbar and it does not include the Help tool (step 6), you can press Shift+F1 and then click on any screen element, including any tool on any toolbar, to see a Help window describing it.**

1 Click on the New Workbook tool to start a new workbook. Click on the Open tool to display the Open dialog box so you can open a workbook from disk. Click on the Save tool to name and save a new workbook—the Save As dialog box appears—or to resave a workbook that you've already named and saved (Chapter 6).

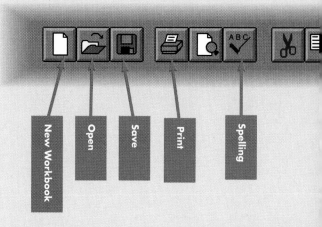

New Workbook · Open · Save · Print · Spelling

6 When you click on the Help tool, the mouse pointer becomes an arrow with a question mark attached. You can then click on any screen element—including a tool on the Standard toolbar—to see a Help window discussing it (Chapter 11).

2 Click on the Print tool to print one copy of the active sheet, bypassing the Print dialog box (Chapter 7).

3 To reverse your most recent action, click on the Undo tool. This is the same as selecting the Undo command from the Edit menu (Chapter 11).

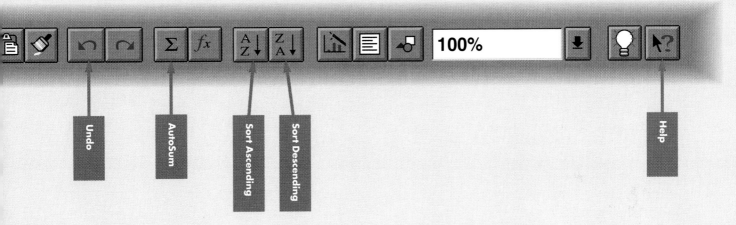

100%

Undo

AutoSum

Sort Ascending

Sort Descending

Help

5 To sort a database (Chapter 14), click on any entry in the column you want to use as the sort key. Then, to sort the database in ascending order, click on the Sort Ascending tool; to sort in descending order, click on the Sort Descending tool. Observe the results carefully. If Excel did not correctly interpret the borders of your database, immediately click on the Undo tool (step 3). Then follow the steps in Chapter 14 to sort the database.

4 Instead of typing the SUM function in a cell (Chapter 4), you can produce this function by activating the cell where you want the sum to appear, clicking on the AutoSum tool, selecting the cells you want to sum, and clicking on the enter box. After you click on the AutoSum tool, cell selection is indicated by dashed lines until you enter the function. Excel even starts you off by selecting the cells it thinks you want to sum; just click on the enter box if Excel guessed right.

How to Issue Commands from the Formatting Toolbar

The Formatting toolbar resides below the Standard toolbar. It offers convenient shortcuts to the most commonly used worksheet formatting commands, sparing you many trips to the Format Cells dialog box (Chapter 9). This page describes only those tools that provide shortcuts to tasks covered in this book.

1 To change the font of the text in the active cell or in all selected cells (Chapter 9), click on the Font drop-down arrow and then click on the desired font.

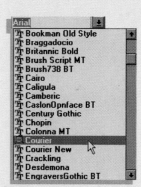

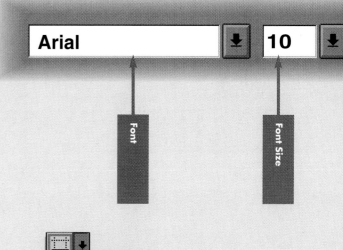

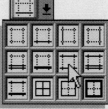

7 To apply the indicated border style to the active cell or to all selected cells (Chapter 9), click on the Borders tool. To apply a different border style, click on the Borders drop-down arrow and click on the style you need.

2 To change the size of the text in the active cell or in all selected cells (Chapter 9), click on the Font Size drop-down arrow and then click on the desired size. Excel measures text size in points, where 72 points equal approximately 1 inch.

3 To boldface, italicize, or underline the text in the active cell or in all selected cells (Chapter 9), click on the Bold, Italic, or Underline tool. Do the same to remove boldface, italics, or underline.

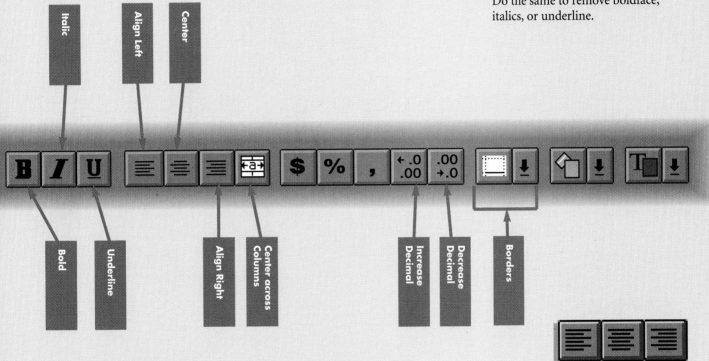

Italic
Align Left
Center
Bold
Underline
Align Right
Center across Columns
Increase Decimal
Decrease Decimal
Borders

4 To change the alignment of cell contents within the active cell or all selected cells (Chapter 9), click on the Align Left, Center, or Align Right tool.

6 To add one decimal place to the number format of the active cell or all selected cells (Chapter 9), click on the Increase Decimal tool. Click on the Decrease Decimal tool to remove one decimal place. Like number formatting commands, these tools affect only the display of numbers in cells, not the underlying numbers used in calculations and shown in the formula bar.

5 Select a cell and, to its right, the cells across which to center the contents of the first cell. Then click on the Center across Columns tool (Chapter 9).

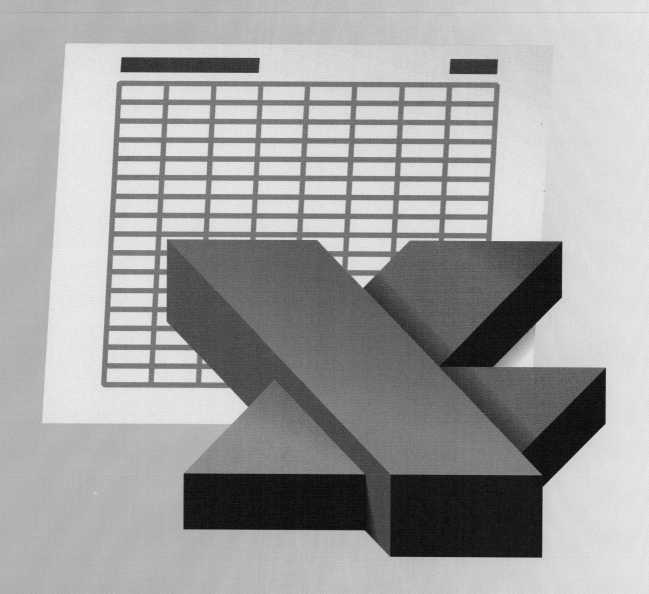

APPENDIX

Installation

 Software is not built into your computer. It is a separate product that someone has to buy and install. In many office situations, an administrator is responsible for installing software on users' machines. Likewise, computers purchased from stores and mail-order firms often come with software such as Excel already installed. Thus, there is a good chance that someone has installed Excel on your machine, and you can skip this appendix.

If you are not sure whether Excel is installed on your computer, follow the steps in Chapter 3 of this book. If you can start Excel, then, plainly, it has been installed.

Microsoft provides clear, complete installation instructions with Excel. These instructions are more than sufficient for most computer users. Moreover, once you start the installation process, you will see on-screen instructions telling you what to do.

This appendix clarifies some of the installation issues that can slow down people who have little computer experience. It gives you the extra knowledge you may need to follow a generally straightforward procedure.

Tips on Installing Excel

The basic installation procedure is simple: You place a disk from your Excel package in a disk drive, and your computer copies information from the disk onto your computer's hard disk. Then you place another disk in the disk drive, the computer copies more information, and so on until the hard disk holds the entire Excel program. There are quite a few variables in the installation process—so many that this book could not possibly discuss them all. Rest assured, however, that for most users in most situations, installation proceeds very smoothly. And the absolute worst thing that can happen if you make a mistake during installation is that you'll have to start over.

TIP SHEET

► Even if you received a shrink-wrapped copy of Excel with your computer, Excel may already be installed. That's because it is more convenient—and perfectly legal—for retailers to install software using an already open copy rather than the copy they give you.

► If your computer has two floppy-disk drives of the same size, you can install Excel from either one. Be sure to use the same one throughout the installation process.

► Your computer may be set to start Windows as soon as it is switched on. In this case you will see *Program Manager* somewhere on your screen. Instead of exiting Windows to display the DOS prompt and perform step 4, you can click on File in the Program Manager menu bar, click on the Run command, type a:\setup or b:\setup depending on what floppy-disk drive holds the Setup disk, and click on the OK button.

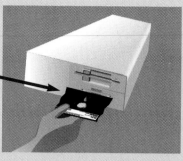

Make sure the disk fits the floppy-disk drive.

1 Your copy of Excel is on either 3.5-inch hard-cased disks or 5.25-inch soft-cased disks. To hold these disks during installation, your computer may have one 3.5-inch floppy-disk drive, one 5.25-inch floppy-disk drive, two drives of the same size, or—the most convenient arrangement—one drive of each size. Contact your software retailer if you don't have a floppy-disk drive of the correct size to accommodate your Excel disks.

9 You can start and use Excel as soon as installation is finished. See Chapter 3 of this book—or read Chapters 1 and 2 for some background information on DOS, Windows, and electronic spreadsheets in general.

8 It can take a while for your computer to read information from the Excel disks. When it's time for you to take out the disk and put in another, your computer will beep at you and tell you what disk it needs. After putting in the next disk, click on OK.

7 If you see this window, then there is not enough room on your hard disk to hold the entire Excel program. You must choose *not* to install certain Excel components, rendering Excel somewhat less capable but still perfectly functional for most purposes. You do this by clicking on the check box of each item you want to omit so that the *x* no longer appears in the box. Then click on Continue. You can omit any component except Microsoft Excel. If the components you omit do not make Excel small enough to fit on your hard disk, you will see this screen again and you will have to omit more components.

2 You need to know the *drive letter* of the floppy-disk drive you'll be using to install Excel. If your computer has only one floppy-disk drive, it is drive A. If your computer has two floppy-disk drives, the top or left drive is drive A and the bottom or right drive is drive B.

Drive A

Drive B

3 One of your Excel disks is labeled *Setup*. To start the installation process, switch on your computer and insert the Setup disk in a floppy-disk drive.

`C:\>win b:\setup`

4 With the DOS prompt displayed on your computer screen, type **win a:\setup** if the Setup disk is in drive A, or **win b:\setup** if the Setup disk is in drive B. Then press the Enter key.

Mouse pointer

Default option

6 What if you see a question that you don't understand—and there's no computer whiz around to help? Just click on the *default* option, an item with a darkened border. The default option is the answer Microsoft thinks you probably want to give, and it's always an answer that can't do your computer any harm.

5 Sit and wait as information is copied from the disk to your computer's hard disk. During installation, on-screen instructions will tell you when to take out one disk and insert another. Periodically you will be asked questions about how you want to install Excel. The questions vary according to such factors as your computer equipment and the amount of empty space on your hard disk. To answer a question, find the answer on the screen and *click* on it. To click on an item means to roll the mouse so that the *mouse pointer* is over the item and then press and immediately release the left mouse button.

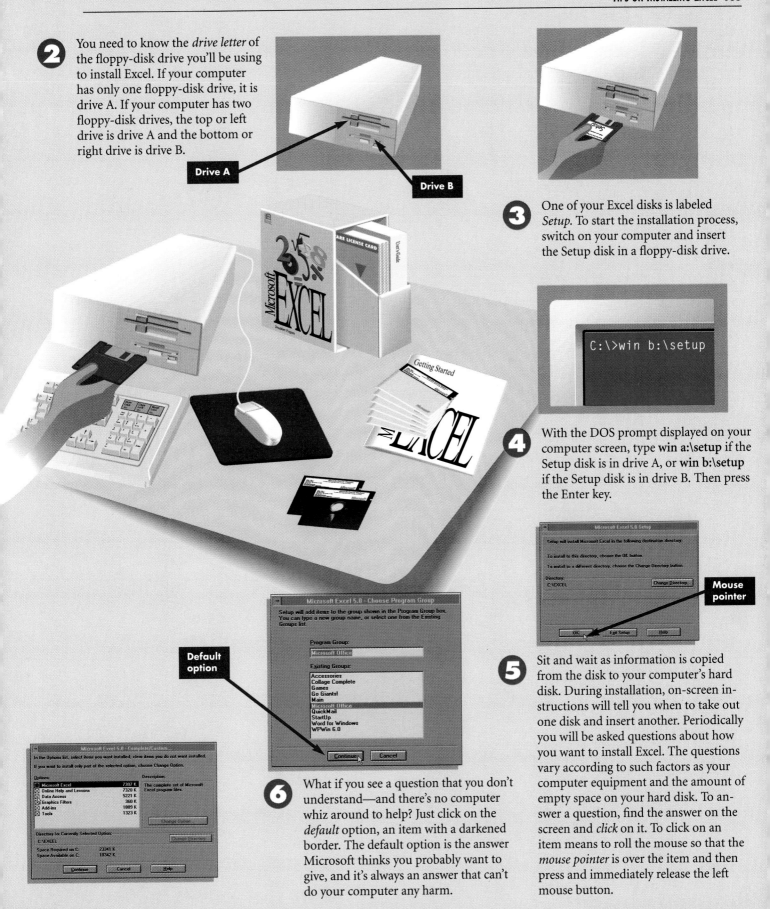

INDEX

SYMBOLS

+ (addition operator), 27

' (apostrophe)

   around special characters, 50

   before labels, 80

: (colon) and summing adjacent cells, 29

, (comma), separating ranges and cell references with, 86

+ (cross), mouse pointer as, 20

/ (division operator), 27

$ (dollar sign)

   before constant cell references, 91, 102

   entering in cell, 76

… (dots) after commands, 16

= (equal sign) for entering formulas, 26, 27

= (equal-to operator) for searching worksheets, 117

=AVERAGE function, 87

=MAX function, 87

=MIN function, 87

=SUM function, 29, 59

! (exclamation point), 50

> (greater-than operator) for searching worksheets, 117

>= (greater-than-or-equal-to operator) for searching worksheets, 117

< (less-than operator) for searching worksheets, 117

<= (less-than-or-equal-to operator) for searching worksheets, 117

* (multiplication operator), 27

<> (not-equal-to operator) for searching worksheets, 117

(overflow markers), 70, 101

% (percent symbol), entering in cell, 76

(pound sign) in format code, 77

) (right parenthesis), 28, 29

; (semicolon) in format code, 77

- (subtraction operator), 27

A

absolute references, 90-91, 102. *See also* cell references

active cell, 21, 25, 32

active document window, 11

Add button (in Spelling dialog box), 99

addition operator (+), 27

Adjust To radio button (for printing), 56

A drive, 42, 135

Align Left tool (on Formatting toolbar), 131

alignment, 80, 131

Alignment tab, 123

   and centering headings over multiple columns, 83, 103

   in Format Cells dialog box, 81

All Files (*.*) option (in Open dialog box), 49

Alt key, 14-15

analysis, what-if, 36-37

apostrophe ('), 50, 80

application window, 10-11, 21

arrow

   field name, 114, 115, 116-117, 123

   mouse pointer as, 69, 103, 124

   next to list, 17

   next to worksheet tabs, 50

   with question mark, mouse pointer as, 96, 128

arrow keys, 15

ascending sort order, 119

AutoFilter command, 114, 116, 117, 123

AutoSum tool versus SUM function, 129

AVERAGE function, 86-87

axis titles, 110-111

B

Back button (in help screen), 97

"Bad command or file name" message, 8

B drive, 42, 135

blank cells, 32

boldface, 74, 75, 102, 124, 131

Bold tool (on Formatting toolbar), 131

Book 1 bar, 21

book1.xls default file name, 43

borders

   adding around cells, 78, 79

   adding from Formatting toolbar, 130, 131

   canceling, 78

buttons on mouse, 12

C

C:\>, 9

c:\>win Setup command, 135

c:\windows\win command, 8

calculations, errors in, 26

cancel box, 25

Cancel button, 16, 17

Can't Undo option (on Edit menu), 95

Caps Lock key, 15, 59

Category list of Format Cells dialog box, 77, 101

Imagination.
Innovation. Insight.

The How It Works Series from Ziff-Davis Press

"... a magnificently seamless integration of text and graphics ..."

Larry Blasko, The Associated Press, reviewing *PC/Computing How Computers Work*

No other books bring computer technology to life like the *How It Works* series from Ziff-Davis Press. Lavish, full-color illustrations and lucid text from some of the world's top computer commentators make *How It Works* books an exciting way to explore the inner workings of PC technology.

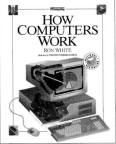

ISBN: 094-7 Price: $22.95

PC/Computing How Computers Work

A worldwide blockbuster that hit the general trade bestseller lists! *PC/Computing* magazine executive editor Ron White dismantles the PC and reveals what really makes it tick.

How Networks Work

Two of the most respected names in connectivity showcase the PC network, illustrating and explaining how each component does its magic and how they all fit together.

ISBN: 129-3 Price: $24.95

How Macs Work

A fun and fascinating voyage to the heart of the Macintosh! Two noted *MacUser* contributors cover the spectrum of Macintosh operations from startup to shutdown.

How Software Works

This dazzlingly illustrated volume from Ron White peeks inside the PC to show in full-color how software breathes life into the PC. Covers Windows™ and all major software categories.

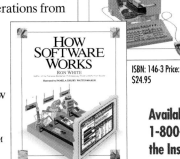

ISBN: 133-1 Price: $24.95

ISBN: 184-6 Price: $17.95

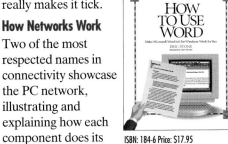

ISBN: 146-3 Price: $24.95

How to Use Your Computer

Conquer computerphobia and see how this intricate machine truly makes life easier. Dozens of full-color graphics showcase the components of the PC and explain how to interact with them.

All About Computers

This one-of-a-kind visual guide for kids features numerous full-color illustrations and photos on every page, combined with dozens of interactive projects that reinforce computer basics, making this an exciting way to learn all about the world of computers.

How To Use Word

Make Word 6.0 for Windows Work for You!

A uniquely visual approach puts the basics of Microsoft's latest Windows-based word processor right before the reader's eyes. Colorful examples invite them to begin producing a variety of documents, quickly and easily. Truly innovative!

How To Use Excel

Make Excel 5.0 for Windows Work for You!

Covering the latest version of Excel, this visually impressive resource guides beginners to spreadsheet fluency through a full-color graphical approach that makes powerful techniques seem plain as day. Hands-on "Try It" sections give new users a chance to sharpen newfound skills.

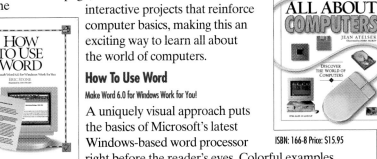

ISBN: 155-2 Price: $22.95

ISBN: 166-8 Price: $15.95

ISBN: 185-4 Price: $17.95

Available at all fine bookstores or by calling 1-800-688-0448, ext. 100. Call for more information on the Instructor's Supplement, including transparencies for each book in the *How It Works* Series.

© 1993 Ziff-Davis Press

Attention Teachers and Trainers
Now You Can
Teach From These Books!

ZD Press now offers instructors and trainers
the materials they need to use these books in their classes.

- An Instructor's Manual features flexible lessons designed for use in a 10- or 15-week course (30-45 course hours).

- Student exercises and tests on floppy disk provide you with an easy way to tailor and/or duplicate tests as you need them.

- A Transparency Package contains all the graphics from the book, each on a single, full-color transparency.

- Spanish edition of *PC/Computing How Computers Work* will be available.

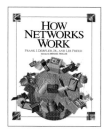